Critical Race Theory

CRITICAL AMERICA
General Editors: Richard Delgado and Jean Stefancic

Recent titles in the Critical America series include:

The First Amendment in Cross-Cultural Perspective:
A Comparative Legal Analysis of the Freedom of Speech
Ronald J. Krotoszynski, Jr.

Feminist Legal Theory: A Primer
Nancy Levit and Robert R. M. Verchick

The Emergence of Mexican America: Recovering Stories
of Mexican Peoplehood in U.S. Culture
John-Michael Rivera

Law and Class in America: Trends since the Cold War
Edited by Paul D. Carrington and Trina Jones

The Sense of Justice: Empathy in Law and Punishment
Markus Dirk Dubber

No Seat at the Table: How Corporate Governance and
Law Keep Women Out of the Boardroom
Douglas M. Branson

White by Law: The Legal Construction of Race,
Revised Edition
Ian Haney López

*Opening the Floodgates: Why America Needs to Rethink
Its Borders and Immigration Laws*
Kevin R. Johnson

*The Reproductive Rights Reader: Law, Medicine,
and the Construction of Motherhood*
Edited by Nancy Ehrenreich

*Chicano Students and the Courts: The Mexican American
Legal Struggle for Educational Equality*
Richard R. Valencia

*Whitewashed: America's Invisible
Middle Eastern Minority*
John Tehranian

American Exceptionalism and International Order
Natsu Taylor Saito

*Critical Race Theory: An Introduction,
Third Edition*
Richard Delgado and Jean Stefancic

For a complete list of titles in the series, please visit the
New York University Press website at www.nyupress.org.

Critical Race Theory

An Introduction

THIRD EDITION

Richard Delgado and Jean Stefancic

FOREWORD BY ANGELA HARRIS

NEW YORK UNIVERSITY PRESS
New York

NEW YORK UNIVERSITY PRESS
New York
www.nyupress.org

References to Internet websites (URLs) were accurate at the time
of writing. Neither the author nor New York University Press is
responsible for URLs that may have expired or changed since
the manuscript was prepared.

Library of Congress Cataloging-in-Publication Data
Names: Delgado, Richard, author. | Stefancic, Jean, author.
Title: Critical race theory : an introduction / Richard Delgado and
Jean Stefancic ; foreword by Angela Harris.
Description: Third edition. | New York : New York University Press,
[2017] | Includes bibliographical references and index.
Identifiers: LCCN 2016047077| ISBN 9781479846368 (cl : alk.
paper) | ISBN 9781479802760 (pb   )
Subjects: LCSH: Race discrimination—Law and legislation—
United States. | Critical legal studies—United States. | United States—
Race relations—Philosophy.
Classification: LCC KF4755 .D454 2017 | DDC 342.7308/73—dc23
LC record available at https://lccn.loc.gov/2016047077

Manufactured in the United States of America

10 9 8 7 6 5 4 3 2 1

Also available as an ebook

Some people see things as they are and say, why?
I dream things that never were and say, why not?
—ROBERT F. KENNEDY,
quoting George Bernard Shaw

In order to get beyond racism, we must first
take account of race. There is no other way.
—JUSTICE HARRY BLACKMUN

Contents

Foreword by Angela Harris xiii

Preface to the Third Edition xix

Acknowledgments xxiii

I Introduction 1
   A. What Is Critical Race Theory? 3
   B. Early Origins 4
   C. Relationship to Previous Movements 5
   D. Principal Figures. 6
   E. Spin-Off Movements 7
   F. Basic Tenets of Critical Race Theory 8
   G. How Much Racism Is There in the World? 11
   H. Organization of This Book. 13
      Questions and Comments for Chapter I. 16
      Suggested Readings 17

II Hallmark Critical Race Theory Themes 19
   A. Interest Convergence, Material Determinism,
      and Racial Realism. 20
   B. Revisionist History. 25
   C. Critique of Liberalism 26

D. Structural Determinism 31
   1. Tools of Thought and the Dilemma of
      Law Reform 32
   2. The Empathic Fallacy 33
   Classroom Exercise 35
   3. Serving Two Masters. 36
   Classroom Exercise 37
   4. Race Remedies Law as a Homeostatic Device . . 38
   Questions and Comments for Chapter II 40
   Suggested Readings 42

III Legal Storytelling and Narrative Analysis 44
A. Opening a Window onto Ignored or
   Alternative Realities 46
B. Counterstorytelling 49
C. Cure for Silencing. 50
D. Storytelling in Court. 52
E. Storytelling on the Defensive 53
   Questions and Comments for Chapter III 55
   Suggested Readings 57

IV Looking Inward 58
A. Intersectionality 58
B. Essentialism and Antiessentialism. 63
C. Nationalism versus Assimilation. 66
   Classroom Exercise 70
D. Racial Mixture. 71
   Questions and Comments for Chapter IV 73
   Suggested Readings 75

V Power and the Shape of Knowledge 77
A. The Black-White Binary 77

B. Critical White Studies...................85
   Classroom Exercise 92
C. Other Developments: Latino and Asian
   Critical Thought, Critical Race Feminism,
   LGBT Theory............................92
   Questions and Comments for Chapter V......98
   Suggested Readings 100

VI Critiques and Responses to Criticism.........102
A. "External" Criticism 102
B. "Internal" Criticism.....................104
   1. The Activist Critiques.................105
   2. Critique of the Intellectual Heart
      of the Movement......................106
C. Critical Race Theory as a Method of Inquiry
   in New Fields and Countries 108
   Classroom Exercise 109
   Questions and Comments for Chapter VI 110
   Suggested Readings 112

VII Critical Race Theory Today 113
A. Right-Wing Offensive....................114
B. Front-Burner Issues 114
   1. Race, Class, Welfare, and Poverty.......115
   2. Policing and Criminal Justice 120
   3. Hate Speech, Language Rights, and
      School Curricula......................125
   4. Affirmative Action and Color Blindness ...130
   5. Globalization and Immigration..........135
   6. Voting Rights 139
C. Identity...............................140
   Classroom Exercise 142

D. Critical Empirical Analysis 142
    Questions and Comments for Chapter VII. . . . 145
    Suggested Readings 149

VIII Conclusion 152
    A. The Future 152
    B. A Critical Race Agenda for the New Century . . 154
    C. Likely Responses to the Critical Race
       Theory Movement 157
       1. Critical Race Theory Becomes the
          New Civil Rights Orthodoxy 157
       2. Critical Race Theory Marginalized
          and Ignored. 158
       3. Critical Race Theory Analyzed
          but Rejected 159
       4. Partial Incorporation. 159
       Classroom Exercise 160
       Questions and Comments for Chapter VIII . . . 162
       Suggested Readings 164

    Glossary of Terms. 167

    Index 187

    About the Authors 199

Foreword

ANGELA HARRIS

In 1982 I was a graduate student in social science at the University of Chicago. I lived at International House, among a vibrant community of American students from African American, Latino/a, South Asian, and other backgrounds, as well as foreign students from Asia, Europe, Africa, and the Americas. We protested and picketed over sanctions for the South African apartheid regime. We saw Michael Jackson moonwalking for the first time on television. Our black male friends got stopped by the police for looking like members of the impoverished African American community that surrounded Hyde Park. We read books in which feminists attacked Freud and Third World women talked back to First World pieties. And we fought with the university administration over our demands for more programs, more resources, and more support for students of color on campus.

In 1983 I was a first-year law student at the University of Chicago. In my entering class of roughly 180 students, there were four African American students, including myself; one Asian American student; and two Latinos. All of our professors were white, and all but two were male.

Even more disorienting, however, than mere demographics was the fact that the lively discourse on racial-ethnic relations, both domestic and international, was gone. None of my professors talked about race or ethnicity; it was apparently irrelevant to the law. None of my professors in the first year talked about feminism or the concerns of women, either. These concerns were also, apparently, irrelevant. Nowhere, in fact, did the cases and materials we read address concerns of group inequality, sexual difference, or cultural identity. There was only one Law, a law that in its universal majesty applied to everyone without regard to race, color, gender, or creed.

Disoriented and unsure of ourselves, a few of us felt that something was profoundly missing in our education, though we could not articulate what the missing something was. We went outside the classroom to look for it. Some of us went to work for the Mandel Legal Aid Clinic. Some of us successfully agitated to get Professor Catharine MacKinnon, the pathbreaking feminist legal scholar, invited to speak (though not invited to join the faculty). Some of us even succeeded in getting permission for Professor Mary Becker to teach a seminar in feminist jurisprudence (though the dean asked us, somewhat bewilderedly, whether men would be excluded from the reading list). In reading groups we began to explore the literature of critical legal studies. But there seemed to be no critical literature on race and the law.

There was, of course, law that had a lot to do with the lives of some communities of color: poverty law, welfare law, criminal law, immigration law. But there was, seemingly, no language in which to embark on a race-based, systematic critique of legal reasoning and legal institutions themselves. As first-year, then second-year, then third-year law students, we had no inkling of the struggles going on at Harvard Law School over the work and teachings of Derrick Bell or of the few scholars—one coauthor of this book among them—who had begun to apply the tools of critical theory to the law. We finished our legal educations never having found a place where the sophisticated discourse of racial critique in which we lived our everyday lives could enter the legal canon.

Three years after I got my law degree, in the summer of 1989, I was a first-year law teacher invited to attend the first-ever workshop on something called "critical race theory," to be held at the St. Benedict Center in Madison, Wisconsin. At that workshop, I discovered what had been missing for me as a student. I met some of the people who, by then, had begun to be recognized across the nation as major intellectual figures: Derrick Bell, Kimberlé Crenshaw, Richard Delgado, Mari Matsuda, Patricia Williams. And I discovered a community of scholars who were inventing a language and creating a literature that was unlike anything I had read for class in three years of law school.

As we enter the twenty-first century, critical race theory is no longer new, but it continues to grow and thrive. The community has expanded: scholars not only from the United States but from countries including Canada, Australia, England, India, and Spain now work within the discipline of critical race theory. The literature has grown in breadth and depth: as this book indicates, not only race-crits but also queer-crits, LatCrits, and critical race feminists seek to reveal and challenge the practices of subordination facilitated and permitted by legal discourse and legal institutions. And, finally, the audience has grown. Critical race theory has exploded from a narrow sub-specialty of jurisprudence chiefly of interest to academic lawyers into a literature read in departments of education, cultural studies, English, sociology, comparative literature, political science, history, and anthropology around the country.

That is where this book comes in. Richard Delgado and Jean Stefancic have written a primer for nonlawyers that makes the now sprawling literature of critical race theory easily accessible to the beginner. From the earliest social and intellectual origins of the movement to its key themes and debates to its methods to its future, Delgado and Stefancic offer a lively, lucid guide to critical race theory and a starting place for further reading and thinking. With the help of this book, even students who find their official course reading lists as barren as I did in 1983 will find their way into a rich and important intellectual debate.

Critical race theory not only dares to treat race as central to the law and policy of the United States; it dares to look beyond the popular belief that getting rid of racism means simply getting rid of ignorance or encouraging everyone to "get along." To read this primer is to be sobered by the recognition that racism is part of the structure of legal institutions but also to be invigorated by the creativity, power, wit, and humanity of the voices speaking about ways to change that structure. As race relations continue to shape our lives in the new century—setting the stage for new tragedies and new hopes—critical race theory has become an indispensable tool for making sense of it all.

Meanwhile, I've saved my 1989 Critical Race Theory Workshop T-shirt. I'm betting it will be worth something someday.

Preface to the Third Edition

Since we published the first edition of this book in 2001, the United States has lived through two economic downturns, an outbreak of terrorism, and the onset of an epidemic of hate directed against newcomers, especially undocumented Latinos and Middle Eastern people. On a more hopeful note, the country elected and reelected its first black president and enacted a comprehensive health-reform measure providing access to health care for many of the formerly uninsured. Gay rights advanced impressively.

The country's demography has changed, as well. Latinos, at about 17 percent of the population, are now the largest minority group, having displaced African Americans, who make up about 13 percent. Asian Americans, although smaller numerically, have increased even more rapidly than the other two larger groups. In California, minorities of color together exceed the white population in size, if not yet in influence. Other states are not far behind.

President Barack Obama's two terms elicited a vigorous response in the form of the Tea Party movement as well as an upsurge in hate speech and opposition to immigration, some of it taking the form of blogs, Internet websites, and talk-radio programs. Globalization, outsourcing, and *maquiladoras* continued to remove tens of thousands of jobs, so that the gap in income and family wealth between the richest few and the rest of society stands at one of the highest levels ever. Police profiling and shootings, the war on drugs, and harsh sentencing policies heightened minority miseries and swelled the prison population. More than fifteen years later, many of these problems remain.

Critical race theory has taken note of all these developments. As the reader will see, a new generation of critical race scholars has examined these issues and more. Employing the same reader-friendly language, absence of buzzwords and jargon, numerous examples, and excerpts from leading court opinions, the third edition brings *Critical Race Theory: An Introduction* up-to-date. The reader will learn about new areas of scholarship, including studies of policing, sentencing, and incarceration; campus climate; workplace pressures; implicit bias; affirmative action; and race and class. Critical race theory continues to spread to other countries; fields, such as sociology, education, philosophy, and religion; and constituencies, such as campus activists. We include new questions for discussion, some of them aimed at posing practical steps that readers can take to advance a progressive race agenda.

Note on Bibliographic Style

We used a modified form of legal (Bluebook) citation style for the items that appear in the Suggested Readings at the end of each chapter. Authors of articles and books appear first in the citation, followed by the title. For an article in a journal, the volume number appears next, followed by the name of the journal and the first page of the article, ending with the year of publication.

RICHARD DELGADO *and* JEAN STEFANCIC
Tuscaloosa, Alabama, 2016

Acknowledgments

We wish to thank the many gallant individuals, historical and contemporary, sung and unsung, who have struggled to make the world a better place. We owe special gratitude to the many writers in the critical race theory, feminist, and critical legal studies communities who have inspired us to think more deeply about social justice than we would have without their teachings. Thanks, as well, to Niko Pfund, past editor in chief at New York University Press, for encouraging us to write this book; to Deborah Gershenowitz, who encouraged us to create a second edition; and to Clara Platter, who prompted us to prepare a third. Anna Frederiksen-Cherry, Peter Lee, Dorothea Reiff, Eugenia Jackson, Jami Vigil, Miriam Garza, and Jessica Lescau supplied editorial and research assistance. The University of Alabama School of Law, Seattle University School of Law, and the University of Colorado Law School provided us with first-rate facilities and an intellectually stimulating work environment. Texas A&M University School of Law and the Institute for Advanced Study provided research support and release time to complete the final edit.

CHAPTER I

Introduction

Think of events that can occur in an ordinary day. A child raises her hand repeatedly in a fourth-grade class; the teacher either recognizes her or does not. A shopper hands a cashier a five-dollar bill to pay for a small item; the clerk either smiles, makes small talk, and deposits change in the shopper's hand or does not. A woman goes to a new-car lot ready to buy; salespeople stand about talking to each other or all converge trying to help her. A jogger in a park gives a brief acknowledgment to an approaching walker; the walker returns the greeting or walks by silently.

You are a white person—the child, the shopper, the jogger. The responses are all from white people and are all negative. Are you annoyed? Do you, for even a moment, think that maybe you are receiving this treatment because of your race? Or might you think that all these people are merely having a bad day? Next suppose that the responses are from people of color. Are you thrown off guard? Angry? Depressed?

You are a person of color and these same things happen to you, and the actors are all white. What is the first thing that comes to your mind? Do you immediately think that you might be treated in these ways because you are not white? If so, how do you feel? Angry? Downcast? Do you let it roll off your back? And if the responses come from fellow people of color, then what do you think? Suppose the person of color is from a group other than your own?

Sometimes actions like these stem from mere rudeness or indifference. The merchant is in a hurry; the walker, lost in thought. But at other times, race seems to play a part. When it does, social scientists call the event a "microaggression," by which they mean one of those many sudden, stunning, or dispiriting transactions that mar the days of women and folks of color. Like water dripping on sandstone, they can be thought of as small acts of racism, consciously or unconsciously perpetrated, welling up from the assumptions about racial matters most of us absorb from the cultural heritage in which we come of age in the United States. These assumptions, in turn, continue to inform our public civic institutions—government, schools, churches— and our private, personal, and corporate lives.

Sometimes the acts are not micro at all. Imagine that the woman or minority standing alone and ignored at the car lot eventually attracts the attention of a salesperson. They negotiate, and she buys a car. Later she learns that she paid almost a thousand dollars more than what the average white male pays for that same car. (See Ian Ayres, Fair Driving, 104 Harv. L. Rev. 817 [1991]; Michael Luo, "Whitening" the Résumé, N.Y. Times, Dec. 5, 2009.) A fourth-grade teacher, shortly before beginning a unit on world cultures, passes out a form asking the children to fill out where their parents "are from." The bright child who raised her hand earlier hesitates, knowing that her parents are undocumented entrants who fear being discovered and deported.

A. What Is Critical Race Theory?

The critical race theory (CRT) movement is a collection of activists and scholars engaged in studying and transforming the relationship among race, racism, and power. The movement considers many of the same issues that conventional civil rights and ethnic studies discourses take up but places them in a broader perspective that includes economics, history, setting, group and self-interest, and emotions and the unconscious. Unlike traditional civil rights discourse, which stresses incrementalism and step-by-step progress, critical race theory questions the very foundations of the liberal order, including equality theory, legal reasoning, Enlightenment rationalism, and neutral principles of constitutional law.

After the first decade, critical race theory began to splinter and now includes a well-developed Asian American jurisprudence, a forceful Latino-critical (LatCrit) contingent, a feisty LGBT interest group, and now a Muslim and Arab caucus. Although the groups continue to maintain good relations under the umbrella of critical race theory, each has developed its own body of literature and set of priorities. For example, Latino and Asian scholars study immigration policy, as well as language rights and discrimination based on accent or national origin. A small group of American Indian scholars addresses indigenous people's rights, sovereignty, and land claims. They also study historical trauma and its legacy and health conse-quences, as well as Indian mascots and co-optation of In-dian culture. Scholars of Middle Eastern and South Asian background address discrimination against their groups, especially in the aftermath of 9/11. (See, e.g., Khaled A. Beydoun, Between Indigence, Islamophobia and Erasure: Poor and Muslim in "War on Terror" America, 105 Calif. L. Rev. ___ [2016]. On the diffusion of critical race theory to other disciplines and nations, see chapter 7.)

B. Early Origins

Critical race theory sprang up in the 1970s, as a number of lawyers, activists, and legal scholars across the coun-try realized, more or less simultaneously, that the heady advances of the civil rights era of the 1960s had stalled and, in many respects, were being rolled back. Realizing that new theories and strategies were needed to combat the subtler forms of racism that were gaining ground, early writers, such as Derrick Bell, Alan Freeman, and Rich-ard Delgado, put their minds to the task. They were soon joined by others, and the group held its first workshop at a convent outside Madison, Wisconsin, in the summer of 1989. Further conferences and meetings took place. Some were closed sessions at which the group threshed out inter-nal problems and struggled to clarify central issues, while others were public, multiday affairs with panels, plenary sessions, keynote speakers, and a broad representation of scholars, students, and activists from a wide variety of disciplines.

C. *Relationship to Previous Movements*

As the reader will see, critical race theory builds on the insights of two previous movements, critical legal studies and radical feminism, to both of which it owes a large debt. It also draws from certain European philosophers and theorists, such as Antonio Gramsci, Michel Foucault, and Jacques Derrida, as well as from the American radical tradition exemplified by such figures as Sojourner Truth, Frederick Douglass, W. E. B. Du Bois, César Chávez, Martin Luther King, Jr., and the Black Power and Chicano movements of the sixties and early seventies. From critical legal studies, the group borrowed the idea of legal indeterminacy—the idea that not every legal case has one correct outcome. Instead, one can decide most cases either way, by emphasizing one line of authority over another or interpreting one fact differently from the way one's adversary does. The group also incorporated skepticism of triumphalist history and the insight that favorable precedent, like *Brown v. Board of Education*, tends to erode over time, cut back by narrow lower-court interpretation, administrative foot dragging, and delay. The group also built on feminism's insights into the relationship between power and the construction of social roles, as well as the unseen, largely invisible collection of patterns and habits that make up patriarchy and other types of domination. From conventional civil rights thought, the movement took a concern for redressing historical wrongs, as well as the insistence that legal and social theory lead to practical consequences. CRT also shared with it a sympathetic understanding of notions of community and group empowerment. From ethnic studies, it took notions such as cultural nationalism, group cohesion, and the need to develop ideas and texts centered around each group and its situation.

D. *Principal Figures*

The late Derrick Bell, formerly at Harvard Law School but serving as visiting professor of law at New York University when he died in 2011, became the movement's intellectual father figure. Most famous for his interest-convergence thesis, Bell authored many of CRT's foundational texts.

Alan Freeman, who taught at the State University of New York at Buffalo Law School, wrote a number of leading articles, including one that documented how the U.S. Supreme Court's race jurisprudence, even when seemingly liberal in thrust, nevertheless legitimized racism. Kimberlé Crenshaw, Angela Harris, Cheryl Harris, Charles Lawrence, Mari Matsuda, and Patricia Williams were major early figures, as well. Leading Asian scholars include Neil Gotanda, Mitu Gulati, Jerry Kang, and Eric Yamamoto. The top American Indian critical scholar is Robert Williams; prolific Latinos of a critical persuasion include Laura Gomez, Ian Haney López, Kevin Johnson, Gerald Lopez, Margaret Montoya, Juan Perea, and Francisco Valdes. Influential black scholars include Paul Butler, Devon Carbado, Lani Guinier, and Angela Onwuachi-Willig. The reader will find their ideas discussed frequently throughout this primer.

The movement counts a number of fellow travelers and writers who are white, notably andré cummings, Nancy Levit, Tom Ross, Jean Stefancic, and Stephanie Wildman. (See also the discussion of critical white studies in chapter 5.)

E. Spin-Off Movements

Although CRT began as a movement in the law, it has rapidly spread beyond that discipline. Today, many scholars in the field of education consider themselves critical race theorists who use CRT's ideas to understand issues of school discipline and hierarchy, tracking, affirmative action, high-stakes testing, controversies over curriculum and history, bilingual and multicultural education, and alternative and charter schools. (See, e.g., Foundations of Critical Race Theory in Education [Edward Taylor, David Gillborn & Gloria Ladson-Billings eds., 2d ed. 2015].) They discuss the rise of biological racism in educational theory and practice and urge attention to the resegregation of American schools. Some question the Anglocentric curriculum and charge that many educators apply a "deficit theory" approach to schooling for minority kids.

Political scientists ponder voting strategies coined by critical race theorists, while women's studies professors teach about intersectionality—the predicament of women of color and others who sit at the intersection of two or more categories. Ethnic studies courses often include a unit on critical race theory, and American studies departments teach material on critical white studies developed by CRT writers. Sociologists, theologians, and health care specialists use critical theory and its ideas. Philosophers incorporate critical race ideas in analyzing issues such as viewpoint discrimination and whether Western philosophy is inherently white in its orientation, values, and method of reasoning.

Unlike some academic disciplines, critical race theory contains an activist dimension. It tries not only to understand our social situation but to change it, setting out not only to ascertain how society organizes itself along racial lines and hierarchies but to transform it for the better. On the spread of critical race theory to other countries, such as Australia, Brazil, India, New Zealand, South Africa, and the United Kingdom, see chapter 7.

F. Basic Tenets of Critical Race Theory

What do critical race theorists believe? Probably not every writer would subscribe to every tenet set out in this book, but many would agree on the following propositions. First, racism is ordinary, not aberrational—"normal science," the usual way society does business, the common, everyday experience of most people of color in this country. Second, most would agree that our system of white-over-color ascendancy serves important purposes, both psychic and material, for the dominant group. The first feature, ordinariness, means that racism is difficult to address or cure because it is not acknowledged. Color-blind, or "formal," conceptions of equality, expressed in rules that insist only on treatment that is the same across the board, can thus remedy only the most blatant forms of discrimination, such as mortgage redlining or an immigration dragnet in a food-processing plant that targets Latino workers or the refusal to hire a black Ph.D. rather than a white college dropout, which stand out and attract our attention.

The second feature, sometimes called "interest convergence" or material determinism, adds a further dimension. Because racism advances the interests of both white elites (materially) and working-class whites (psychically), large segments of society have little incentive to eradicate it. Consider, for example, Derrick Bell's shocking proposal (discussed in chapter 2) that *Brown v. Board of Education*—considered a great triumph of civil rights litigation—may have resulted more from the self-interest of elite whites than from a desire to help blacks.

A third theme of critical race theory, the "social construction" thesis, holds that race and races are products of social thought and relations. Not objective, inherent, or fixed, they correspond to no biological or genetic reality; rather, races are categories that society invents, manipulates, or retires when convenient. People with common origins share certain physical traits, of course, such as skin color, physique, and hair texture. But these constitute only an extremely small portion of their genetic endowment, are dwarfed by what we have in common, and have little or nothing to do with distinctly human, higher-order traits, such as personality, intelligence, and moral behavior. That society frequently chooses to ignore these scientific truths, creates races, and endows them with pseudo-permanent characteristics is of great interest to critical race theory.

Another, somewhat more recent, development concerns differential racialization and its consequences. Critical writers in law, as well as in social science, have drawn attention to the ways the dominant society racializes different minority groups at different times, in response to shifting needs such as the labor market. At one period, for example, society may have had little use for blacks but much need for Mexican or Japanese agricultural workers. At another time, the Japanese, including citizens of long standing, may have been in intense disfavor and removed to war relocation camps, while society cultivated other groups of color for jobs in war industry or as cannon fodder on the front. In one era, Muslims are somewhat exotic neighbors who go to mosques and pray several times of day—harmless but odd. A few years later, they emerge as security threats.

Popular images and stereotypes of various minority groups shift over time, as well. In one era, a group of color may be depicted as happy-go-lucky, simpleminded, and content to serve white folks. A little later, when conditions change, that very same group may appear in cartoons, movies, and other cultural scripts as menacing, brutish, and out of control, requiring close supervision. In one age, Middle Eastern people are exotic, fetishized figures wearing veils, wielding curved swords, and summoning genies from lamps. Later, after circumstances change, they emerge as fanatical, religiously crazed terrorists bent on destroying America and killing innocent citizens.

Closely related to differential racialization—the idea that each race has its own origins and ever-evolving history—is the notion of intersectionality and antiessentialism. No person has a single, easily stated, unitary identity. A white feminist may also be Jewish or working class or a single mother. An African American activist may be male or female, gay or straight. A Latino may be a Democrat, a Republican, or even black—perhaps because that person's family hails from the Caribbean. An Asian may be a recently arrived Hmong of rural background and unfamiliar with mercantile life or a fourth-generation Chinese with a father who is a university professor and a mother who operates a business. Everyone has potentially conflicting, overlapping identities, loyalties, and allegiances.

A final element concerns the notion of a unique voice of color. Coexisting in somewhat uneasy tension with anti-essentialism, the voice-of-color thesis holds that because of their different histories and experiences with oppression, black, American Indian, Asian, and Latino writers and thinkers may be able to communicate to their white counterparts matters that the whites are unlikely to know. Minority status, in other words, brings with it a presumed competence to speak about race and racism. The "legal storytelling" movement urges black and brown writers to recount their experiences with racism and the legal system and to apply their own unique perspectives to assess law's master narratives. This topic, too, is taken up later in this book.

G. *How Much Racism Is There in the World?*

Many modern-day readers believe that racism is declining or that class today is more important than race. And it is certainly true that lynching and other shocking expressions of racism are less frequent than in the past. Moreover, many Euro-Americans consider themselves to have black,

Latino, or Asian friends. Many enjoy watching black or Latino entertainers and sports figures and listening to rap music. Still, by every social indicator, racism continues to blight the lives of people of color, including holders of high-echelon jobs, even judges. Police-community encounters are daily reminders that this continues to happen.

> I concede that I am black. I do not apologize for that obvious fact. I take rational pride in my heritage, just as most other ethnics take pride in theirs. However, that one is black does not mean . . . that he is anti-white. . . . As do most blacks, I believe that the corridors of history in this country have been lined with countless instances of racial injustice. . . .
>
> Thus a threshold question which might be inferred from defendants' petition is: Since blacks (like most other thoughtful Americans) are aware of the "sordid chapter in American history" of racial injustice, shouldn't black judges be disqualified per se from adjudicating cases involving claims of racial discrimination?
>
> *Federal Judge Leon Higginbotham, in refusing to disqualify himself from hearing a case, Commonwealth v. Local Union 542, International Union of Operating Engineers, 388 F. Supp. 155, 163, 165 (E.D. Pa. 1974)*

Studies show that blacks and Latinos who seek loans, apartments, or jobs are much more apt than similarly qualified whites to suffer rejections, often for vague or spurious reasons. Even highly placed black or Latino lawyers or executives may attract suspicion while riding a commuter train or upon arriving at their offices earlier than usual. The prison population is largely black and brown; chief executive officers, senators, surgeons, and university presidents are almost all white. In recent years, almost all Oscar-winning actors have been white. Poverty, however, has a black or brown face: black families command, on the average, about one-thirteenth of the assets of their white counterparts. They pay more for many products and services, including cars. People of color lead shorter lives, receive worse medical care, complete fewer years of school, and occupy more menial jobs than do whites. A recent United Nations report showed that African Americans in the United States would make up the twenty-seventh-ranked nation in the world on a combined index of social well-being; Latinos would rank thirty-third. Studies using the Implicit Association Test (IAT) show that a large percentage of American citizens harbor negative attitudes toward members of groups other than their own. Why all this is so and the relationship between racism and economic oppression—between race and class—are topics of great interest to critical race theory and are covered later in this book.

H. Organization of This Book

Critical Race Theory: An Introduction addresses, in simple, straightforward language, the foregoing and additional ideas characteristic of critical race jurisprudence. Chapter 2 presents four large themes in that body of thought—interest convergence or material determinism, revisionist interpretations of history, the critique of liberalism, and structural determinism.

Chapter 3 takes up storytelling, counterstorytelling, and the narrative turn in general; chapter 4 addresses the twin themes of intersectionality and antiessentialism. It also considers cultural nationalism and its opposite—the idea that minorities should attempt to assimilate and blend into mainstream society. Do immigrants weaken American solidarity and identity?

Does American racial thought contain an implicit black-white binary, an unstated dichotomy in which society comes divided into two groups, whites and blacks, so that nonblack minority groups, such as Filipinos or Puerto Ricans, enter into the equation only insofar as they are able to depict themselves and their problems by analogy to blacks? Chapter 5 explores this issue, as well as whiteness studies. Social scientists have long put minority groups under the lens, examining their culture, intelligence, motivation, family arrangements, music, and much more. Recently scholars on both sides of the color line have switched perspective and are examining whites as a group. One topic that critical white studies addresses is whether such a thing as white privilege exists and, if so, what it consists of. Chapter 5 also looks at the scholarship of other racial groups such as LatCrits, critical Asian writers, feminists, and LGBT theorists.

As the reader might imagine, critical race theory has come in for its share of criticism. Chapter 6 examines the main challenges that writers from both the Left and the Right have leveled at this approach to civil rights. It also includes responses to those objections. Chapter 7 describes critical race theory's current situation. It also ponders a few of the issues on the movement's agenda, including hate speech, campus climate, criminal justice, racial profiling, merit, affirmative action, poverty, immigration, national security, and globalization. A concluding chapter hazards some predictions on the country's racial future and CRT's role in it.

The reader will find in each chapter questions for discussion and a short list of suggested readings. We include hypotheticals and classroom exercises where we think these will promote understanding. We also excerpt passages from judicial decisions illustrating the influence of critical race theory. At the end, we include an extensive glossary of terms, including many that are not found in this book.

QUESTIONS AND COMMENTS FOR CHAPTER 1

1. Is critical race theory pessimistic? Consider that it holds that racism is ordinary, normal, and embedded in society and, moreover, that changes in relationships among the races (which include both improvements and turns for the worse) reflect the interest of dominant groups, rather than idealism, altruism, or the rule of law. Or is it optimistic, because it believes that race is a social construction? (As such, it should be subject to ready change.)

1. And if CRT does have a dark side, what follows from that? Is medicine pessimistic because it focuses on diseases and traumas?

2. Most people of color believe that the world contains much more racism than white folks do. What accounts for this difference?

3. Is race or class more important in determining one's life chances?

4. Why have scholars in the field of education, particularly, found CRT's teachings helpful?

5. Is racism essentially a cognitive error—a product of ignorance or lack of experience—and so correctable through teaching and learning?

6. If you are a community activist, what lessons from this chapter could you apply to your daily work?

7. Have you read any books, published before 1989 perhaps, that were works of critical race theory, even if they were not designated as such?

SUGGESTED READINGS

Ayres, Ian, Pervasive Discrimination: Unconventional Evidence of Racial and Gender Discrimination (2003).

Bell, Derrick A., Race, Racism, and American Law (6th ed. 2008).

Bonilla-Silva, Eduardo, Color-Blind Racism and the Persistence of Racial Inequality in America (3d ed. 2009).

Carbado, Devon W. & Mitu Gulati, Acting White: Rethinking Race in "Post-Racial" America (2013; repr., 2015).

Cho, Sumi & Robert Westley, Critical Race Coalitions: Key Movements That Performed the Theory, 33 U.C. Davis L. Rev. 1377 (2000).

Critical Race Studies in Education Association, http://www.crseassoc.org/ (official website).

Critical Race Theory: The Cutting Edge (Richard Delgado & Jean Stefancic eds., 3d ed. 2013).

Critical Race Theory: The Key Writings That Formed the Movement (Kimberlé Crenshaw, Neil Gotanda, Gary Peller & Kendall Thomas eds., 1995).

Critical Race Theory in Education: All God's Children Got a Song (Adrienne D. Dixson, Celia D. Rousseau & Jamel K. Donnor eds., 2d ed. 2016).

Curry, Tommy, Will the Real CRT Please Stand Up? 2 The Crit: J. Crit. Legal Stud. 1 (2009).

Delgado, Richard, Liberal McCarthyism and the Origins of Critical Race Theory, 94 Iowa L. Rev. 1505 (2009).

Edelman, Benjamin G., Michael Luca & Daniel Svirsky,
    Racial Discrimination in the Sharing Economy (Har-
    vard Business School Working Paper, Jan. 6, 2016).
Gelber, Katharine & Luke McNamara, The Effects of
    Civil Hate Speech Laws: Lessons from Australia, 49
    Law & Society Rev. 631 (2015).
Haney López, Ian F., The Social Construction of Race:
    Some Observations on Illusion, Fabrication, and
    Choice, 29 Harv. C.R.-C.L. L. Rev. 1 (1994).
Moschel, Mathias, Law, Lawyers and Race: Critical Race
    Theory from the United States to Europe (2014).
Omi, Michael & Howard Winant, Racial Formation in
    the United States (3d ed. 2014).
Perea, Juan F., Buscando América: Why Integration and
    Equal Protection Fail to Protect Latinos, 117 Harv. L.
    Rev. 1420 (2004).
Race and Races: Cases and Resources for a Diverse
    America (Juan Perea, Richard Delgado, Angela Harris,
    Jean Stefancic & Stephanie Wildman eds., 3d ed. 2015).
Race Is . . . Race Isn't: Critical Race Theory and Qualita-
    tive Studies in Education (Laurence Park, Donna Deyhle
    & Sofia Villenas eds., 1999).
Trubek, David, M., Foundational Events, Foundational
    Myths, and the Creation of Critical Race Theory,
    or How to Get Along with a Little Help from Your
    Friends, 43 Conn. L. Rev. 1503 (2011).

CHAPTER II

Hallmark Critical Race Theory Themes

Imagine that a pair of businessmen pass a beggar on a busy downtown street. One says something disparaging about "those bums always sticking their hands out—I wish they would get a job." His friend takes him to task for his display of classism. He explains that the street person may have overheard the remark and had his feelings hurt. He points out that we should all strive to purge ourselves of racism, classism, and sexism, that thoughts have consequences, and that how you speak makes a difference. The first business-man mutters something about political correctness and makes a mental note not to let his true feelings show in front of his friend again. Is the beggar any better off?

Or imagine that a task force of highly advanced extrater-restrials lands on Earth and approaches the nearest human being they can find, who happens to be a street person relaxing on a park bench. They offer him any one of three magic potions. The first is a pill that will rid the world of sexism—demeaning, misogynist attitudes toward women. The second is a pill that will cure racism; the third, one that will cure classism—negative attitudes toward people of lower socioeconomic station than oneself. Introduced into the planet's water system, each pill will cure one of the three scourges effectively and permanently. The street person, of course, chooses classism and throws pill number three into a nearby water department reservoir.

Will the lives of poor people like him improve very much the next day? Perhaps not. Passersby may be somewhat kinder, may smile at them more often, but if something inherent in the nature of our capitalist system ineluctably produces poverty and class segregation, that system will continue to create and chew up victims, irrespective of our attitudes toward them. Individual street people may feel better, but they will still be street people. And the free-enterprise system, which is built on the idea of winners and losers, will continue to produce new ones every day.

What about racism? Suppose a magic pill like the one mentioned above were invented, or perhaps an enterprising entrepreneur developed The Ultimate Diversity Seminar, one so effective that it would completely eliminate unkind thoughts, stereotypes, and misimpressions harbored by its participants toward persons of other races. The president's civil rights adviser prevails on all the nation's teachers to introduce it into every K–12 classroom, and on the major television networks and cable network news to show it on prime time.

Would life improve very much for people of color?

A. Interest Convergence, Material Determinism, and Racial Realism

This hypothetical question poses an issue that squarely divides critical race theory thinkers—indeed, civil rights activists in general. One camp, which we may call "idealists," holds that racism and discrimination are matters of thinking, mental categorization, attitude, and discourse. Race is a social construction, not a biological reality, they reason. Hence we may unmake it and deprive it of much of its sting by changing the system of images, words, attitudes, unconscious feelings, scripts, and social teachings by which we convey to one another that certain people are less intelligent, reliable, hardworking, virtuous, and American than others.

A contrasting school—the "realists" or economic determinists—holds that though attitudes and words are important, racism is much more than a collection of unfavorable impressions of members of other groups. For realists, racism is a means by which society allocates privilege and status. Racial hierarchies determine who gets tangible benefits, including the best jobs, the best schools, and invitations to parties in people's homes. Members of this school of thought point out that antiblack prejudice sprang up with slavery and capitalists' need for labor. Before then, educated Europeans held a generally positive attitude toward Africans, recognizing that African civilizations were highly advanced with vast libraries and centers of learning. Indeed, North Africans pioneered mathematics, medicine, and astronomy long before Europeans had much knowledge of these disciplines.

Materialists point out that conquering nations universally demonize their subjects to feel better about exploiting them, so that, for example, planters and ranchers in Texas and the Southwest circulated notions of Mexican inferiority at roughly the same period that they found it necessary to take over Mexican lands or, later, to import Mexican people for backbreaking labor. For materialists, understanding the ebb and flow of racial progress and retrenchment requires a careful look at conditions prevailing at different times in history. Circumstances change so that one group finds it possible to seize advantage or to exploit another. They do so and then form appropriate collective attitudes to rationalize what was done. Moreover, what is true for subordination of minorities is also true for its relief: civil rights gains for communities of color coincide with the dictates of white self-interest. Little happens out of altruism alone.

In the early years of critical race theory, the realists were in a large majority. For example, scholars questioned whether the much-vaunted system of civil rights remedies ended up doing people of color much good. In a classic article in the *Harvard Law Review*, Derrick Bell argued that civil rights advances for blacks always seemed to coincide with changing economic conditions and the self-interest of elite whites. Sympathy, mercy, and evolving standards of social decency and conscience amounted to little, if anything. Audaciously, Bell selected *Brown v. Board of Education*, the crown jewel of U.S. Supreme Court jurisprudence, and invited his readers to ask themselves why the American legal system suddenly, in 1954, opened up as it did. The NAACP Legal Defense Fund had been courageously and tenaciously litigating school desegregation cases for years, usually losing or, at best, winning narrow victories.

In 1954, however, the Supreme Court unexpectedly gave them everything they wanted. Why just then? Bell hypothesized that world and domestic considerations—not moral qualms over blacks' plight—precipitated the pathbreaking decision. By 1954 the country had ended the Korean War; the Second World War was not long past. In both wars, African American soldiers had performed valiantly in the service of democracy. Many of them returned to the United States, having experienced for the first time in their lives a setting in which cooperation and survival took precedence over racism. They were unlikely to return willingly to regimes of menial labor and social vilification. For the first time in years, the possibility of mass domestic unrest loomed.

During that period, as well, the United States was locked in the Cold War, a titanic struggle with the forces of international communism for the loyalties of uncommitted emerging nations, most of which were black, brown, or Asian. It would ill serve the U.S. interest if the world press continued to carry stories of lynchings, Klan violence, and racist sheriffs. It was time for the United States to soften its stance toward domestic minorities. The interests of whites and blacks, for a brief moment, converged.

Bell's article evoked outrage and accusations of cynicism. Yet, years later, the legal historian Mary Dudziak carried out extensive archival research in the files of the U.S. Department of State and the U.S. Department of Justice. Analyzing foreign press reports, as well as letters from U.S. ambassadors abroad, she showed that Bell's intuition was largely correct. When the Justice Department intervened on the side of the NAACP for the first time in a major school-desegregation case, it was responding to a flood of secret cables and memos outlining the United States' interest in improving its image in the eyes of the Third World.

Since Bell first propounded interest convergence, critical race theorists have applied it to understand many of the twists and turns of minority legal history, including that of Latinos. (See, e.g., Richard Delgado, Rodrigo's Roundelay: Hernandez v. Texas and the Interest-Convergence Dilemma, 41 Harv. C.R.-C.L. L. Rev. 23 [2006].) Others have sought to apply it to the current world situation as the United States struggles to strengthen the hand of moderate Islam vis-à-vis its more fundamentalist faction.

American leadership in the 21st century. . . . means a wise application of military power, and rallying the world behind causes that are right. . . . That's why I will keep working to shut down the prison at Guantanamo. It is expensive, unnecessary, and only serves as a recruitment brochure for our enemies. . . .

The world respects us not just for our arsenal; it respects us for our diversity, and our openness, and the way we respect every faith. . . .

His Holiness, Pope Francis, told this body from the very spot that I'm standing on tonight that "to imitate the hatred and violence of tyrants and murderers is the best way to take their place." When politicians insult Muslims, whether abroad or our fellow citizens, when a mosque is vandalized, or a kid is called names . . . that's . . . just wrong. It diminishes us in the eyes of the world. It makes it harder to achieve our goals. It betrays who we are as a country.

President Barack Obama, State of the Union address, 2016

B. Revisionist History

Derrick Bell's analysis of *Brown* illustrates a second signature CRT theme. Revisionist history reexamines America's historical record, replacing comforting majoritarian interpretations of events with ones that square more accurately with minorities' experiences. It also offers evidence, sometimes suppressed, in that very record, to support those new interpretations. Revisionist historians often strive to unearth little-known chapters of racial struggle, sometimes in ways that reinforce current reform efforts. (See, e.g., *Lobato v. Taylor* and *Mabo v. Queensland*, two land-reform cases cited in chapter 5.) Revisionism is often materialist in thrust, holding that to understand the zigs and zags of black, Latino, and Asian fortunes, one must look to matters like profit, labor supply, international relations, and the interest of elite whites. For the realists, attitudes follow, explain, and rationalize what is taking place in the material sector.

The difference between the materialists and the idealists is no minor matter. It shapes strategy on decisions of how and where to invest one's energies. If the materialists are right, one needs to change the physical circumstances of minorities' lives before racism will abate. One takes seriously things like unions, immigration quotas, the prison-industrial complex, and the loss of manufacturing and service jobs to outsourcing. If one is an idealist, campus speech codes, tort remedies for racist speech, media stereotypes, diversity seminars, healing circles, Academy Awards, and increasing the representation of black, brown, and

Asian actors on television shows will be high on one's list of priorities. A middle ground would see both forces, material and cultural, operating together so that race reformers working in either area contribute to a broad program of racial reform.

> Racial insults are in no way comparable to statements such as, "You are a God damned . . . liar," which [a standard guide] gives as an example of a "mere insult." Racial insults are different qualitatively because they conjure up the entire history of racial discrimination in this country.
>
> *Taylor v. Metzger, 706 A. 2d 685, 695 (N.J. 1998), citing Richard Delgado, Words That Wound: A Tort Action for Racial Insults, Epithets, and Name-Calling, 17 Harv. C.R.-C.L. L. Rev. 133, 157 (1982)*

C. Critique of Liberalism

As mentioned earlier, critical race scholars are discontented with liberalism as a framework for addressing America's racial problems. Many liberals believe in color blindness and neutral principles of constitutional law. They believe in equality, especially equal treatment for all persons, regardless of their different histories or current situations. Some even managed to convince themselves that with the election of Barack Obama, we arrived at a postracial stage of social development.

> The white race deems itself to be the dominant race in this country. And so it is, in prestige, in achievements, in education, in wealth, and in power. . . . But in view of the constitution, in the eye of the law, there is in this country no superior,

dominant, ruling class of citizens. There is no caste here. Our constitution is color-blind, and neither knows nor tolerates classes among citizens. In respect of civil rights, all citizens are equal before the law. The humblest is the peer of the most powerful.

Justice John Harlan, dissenting, in Plessy v. Ferguson, 163 U.S. 537, 545 (1896)

Color blindness can be admirable, as when a governmental decision maker refuses to give in to local prejudices. But it can be perverse, for example, when it stands in the way of taking account of difference in order to help people in need. An extreme version of color blindness, seen in certain Supreme Court opinions today, holds that it is wrong for the law to take any note of race, even to remedy a historical wrong. Critical race theorists (or "crits," as they are sometimes called) hold that color blindness of the latter forms will allow us to redress only extremely egregious racial harms, ones that everyone would notice and condemn. But if racism is embedded in our thought processes and social structures as deeply as many crits believe, then the "ordinary business" of society—the routines, practices, and institutions that we rely on to do the world's work—will keep minorities in subordinate positions. Only aggressive, color-conscious efforts to change the way things are will do much to ameliorate misery. As an example of one such strategy, one critical race scholar proposed that society "look to the bottom" in judging new laws. If they would not relieve the distress of the poorest group—or, worse, if they compound it—we should reject them. Although color blindness seems firmly entrenched in the judiciary, a few judges have made exceptions in unusual circumstances.

> We are mindful that the Supreme Court has rejected the "role model" argument for reverse discrimination. . . . The argument for the black lieutenant is not of that character. We doubt that many inmates of boot camps aspire to become correctional officers, though doubtless some do. . . . The black lieutenant is needed because the black inmates are believed unlikely to play the correctional game of brutal drill sergeant and brutalized recruit unless there are some blacks in authority in the camp. This is not just speculation, but is backed up by expert evidence that the plaintiffs did not rebut. The defendants' experts . . . did not rely on generalities about racial balance or diversity; did not, for that matter, defend a goal of racial balance. They opined that the boot camp in Greene County would not succeed in its mission of pacification and reformation with as white a staff as it would have had if a black male had not been appointed to one of the lieutenant slots. For then a security staff less than 6 percent black (4 out of 71), with no male black supervisor, would be administering a program for a prison population almost 70 percent black. . . .
>
> We hold . . . that . . . the preference that the administration of the Greene County boot camp gave a black male applicant for a lieutenant's job on the ground of his race was not unconstitutional.
>
> *Judge Richard Posner, Wittmer v. Peters, 87 F.3d 916, 919–20 (7th Cir. 1996)*

Crits are suspicious of another liberal mainstay, namely, rights. Particularly some of the older, more radical CRT scholars with roots in racial realism and an economic view of history believe that moral and legal rights are apt to do the right holder much less good than we like to think. In our system, rights are almost always procedural (for example, to a fair process) rather than substantive (for example, to food, housing, or education). Think how that system applauds affording everyone equality of opportunity but resists programs that assure equality of results, such as affirmative action at an elite college or university or efforts to equalize public school funding among districts in a region. Moreover, rights are almost always cut back when they conflict with the interests of the powerful. For example, hate speech, which targets mainly minorities, gays, lesbians, and other outsiders, receives legal protection, while speech that offends the interests of empowered groups finds a ready exception in First Amendment law. Think, for example, of speech that insults a judge or other authority figure, that defames a wealthy and well-regarded person, that divulges a government secret, or that deceptively advertises products, thus cheating a large class of middle-income consumers. Think of speech that violates the copyright of a powerful publishing house or famous author.

Moreover, rights are said to be alienating. They separate people from each other—"stay away, I've got my rights"—rather than encouraging them to form close, respectful communities. And with civil rights, lower courts have found it easy to narrow or distinguish the broad, ringing landmark decision like *Brown v. Board of Education*. The group that supposedly benefits always greets cases like *Brown* with great celebration. But after the singing and dancing die down, the breakthrough is quietly cut back by narrow interpretation, administrative obstruction, or delay. In the end, the minority group is left little better than it was before, if not worse. Its friends, the liberals, believing the problem has been solved, go on to a different campaign, such as saving the whales, while its adversaries, the conservatives, furious that the Supreme Court has given way once again to undeserving minorities, step up their resistance. (See Gerald N. Rosenberg, The Hollow Hope: Can Courts Bring About Social Change? [2d ed. 2008].)

Lest the reader think that the crits are too hard on well-meaning liberals, bear in mind that in recent years the movement has softened somewhat. When it sprang up in the 1970s, complacent, backsliding liberalism represented the principal impediment to racial progress. Today that obstacle has been replaced by rampant, in-your-face conservatism that co-opts Martin Luther King, Jr.'s language; finds little use for welfare, affirmative action, or other programs vital to the poor and minorities; and wants to militarize the border and make everyone speak English when businesses are crying for workers with foreign-language proficiency.

Other conservatives have seized on President Barack Obama's election to declare that America is now a post-racial society, so that it is time for blacks and other minorities to stop complaining and roll up their sleeves like anyone else. Welfare payments, they say, merely create dependency and idleness. Because most critical race theorists believe things are more complicated than that, many of them have stopped focusing on liberalism and its ills and have begun to address the conservative tide. And a determined group maintains that rights are not a snare and a delusion; rather, they can bring genuine gains, while the struggle to obtain them unifies the group in a sense of common venture.

D. Structural Determinism

Everyone has heard the story about Eskimo languages, some of which supposedly contain many words for different kinds of snow. Imagine the opposite predicament—a society that has only one word (say, "racism") for a phenomenon that is much more complex than that, for example, biological racism; intentional racism; unconscious racism; microaggressions; nativism; institutional racism; racism tinged with homophobia or sexism; racism that takes the form of indifference, coldness, or implicit associations; and white privilege, reserving favors, smiles, kindness, the best stories, one's most charming side, and invitations to real intimacy for one's own kind or class.

Or imagine a painter raised by parents and preschool teachers who teach him that the world contains only three colors, red, blue, and yellow; or a would-be writer who is raised with an artificially low vocabulary of three hundred words. Children raised in smoggy Mexico City are said to paint pictures with a brownish-yellow, never blue, sky. These examples point out the concept that lies at the heart of structural determinism, the idea that our system, by reason of its structure and vocabulary, is ill equipped to redress certain types of wrong. Structural determinism, a powerful notion that engages both the idealistic and the materialistic strands of critical race theory, takes a number of forms. Consider the following four. (A fifth, the black-white binary, comes in for discussion in chapter 5.)

1. Tools of Thought and the Dilemma of Law Reform

Traditional legal research tools, found in standard law libraries, rely on a series of headnotes, index numbers, and other categories that lawyers use to find precedent. (With computerization, this reliance is somewhat less acute than it was formerly, but the problem still persists.) Suppose that no case is on point because the lawyer faces a problem of first impression—the first of its kind—requiring legal innovation. In such situations, commercial research tools will lead the lawyer to dead ends—to solutions that have not worked. What the situation calls for is innovation, not the application of some preexisting rule or category. Even when a new idea, such as jury nullification, was beginning to catch on, the legal indexers who compiled the reference books and indexing tools may have failed to realize its significance. When Sir William Blackstone's *Commentaries on the Laws of England* laid down the basic structure of liberal/capitalist thought, this served as a template for future generations of lawyers, so that legal change thereafter came slowly. Once the structure of law and legal categories takes form, it replicates itself much as, in the world of biology, DNA enables organisms to replicate. In some respects, the predicament is the old one about the chicken and the egg. It is hard to think about something that has no name, and it is difficult to name something unless one's interpretive community has begun talking and thinking about it.

As a thought exercise, the reader is invited to consider how many of the following terms and ideas, mentioned in this book and highly relevant to the work of progressive lawyers and activists, are apt to be found in standard legal reference works: intersectionality, interest convergence, microaggressions, antiessentialism, hegemony, hate speech, language rights, black-white binary, jury nullification. How long will it take before these concepts enter the official vocabulary of law?

2. The Empathic Fallacy

Consider how in certain controversies, for example, the one over hate speech, a particular type of tough-minded participant is apt to urge a free-market response: if a minority finds himself or herself on the receiving end of a stinging remark, the solution, it is said, is not to punish the speaker or to enact some kind of campus hate-speech rule but to urge the victim to speak back to the offender. "The cure for bad speech is more speech."

One difficulty with this approach is that it may be physically dangerous to talk back. Much hate speech is uttered in several-on-one situations, where talking back would be foolhardy. At other times, it is delivered in anonymous or cowardly fashion, such as graffiti scrawled on the bulletin board of a minority-student group or an unsigned note in the mailbox of a student of color. In these instances, more speech is, of course, impossible.

But a more basic problem is that much hate speech is simply not perceived as such at the time. The history of racial depiction shows that our society has blithely consumed a shocking parade of Sambos, coons, sneaky Japanese, exotic Orientals, and indolent, napping Mexicans—images that society perceived at the time as amusing, cute, or, worse yet, true. How can one talk back to messages, scripts, and stereotypes that are embedded in the minds of one's fellow citizens and, indeed, the national psyche? Trying to do so makes one come across as humorless or touchy. The idea that one can use words to undo the meanings that others attach to these very same words is to commit the empathic fallacy—the belief that one can change a narrative by merely offering another, better one—that the reader's or listener's empathy will quickly and reliably take over. (See Richard Delgado & Jean Stefancic, Images of the Outsider in American Law and Culture: Can Free Expression Remedy Systemic Social Ills?, 77 Cornell L. Rev. 1258 [1992].)

Unfortunately, however, empathy is in shorter supply than we think. Most people in their daily lives do not come into contact with many persons of radically different race or social station. We converse with, and read materials written by, persons in our own cultures. In some sense, we are all our stock of narratives—the terms, preconceptions, scripts, and understandings that we use to make sense of the world. They constitute who we are, the basis on which we judge new narratives—such as one about an African American who is a genius or a hardworking Chicano who holds three jobs. The idea that a better, fairer script can readily substitute for the older, prejudiced one is attractive but is falsified by history. Change comes slowly. Try explaining to someone who has never seen a Mexican, except for cartoon figures wearing sombreros and serapes, that most Mexicans wear business suits.

One of the reasons for avoiding excessive sentences is that the empathy required of . . . citizens in a democracy . . . is stunted when parents are away in prison. "[W]ithout regular comforting, physical contact and sensory stimulation from birth, the biological capacity for sociality—the precondition for empathy and conscience—cannot develop . . . and [e]mpathy requires the nurturing required by early social relationships." Breaking up families by sending fathers and mothers to prison for unnecessarily long terms sows the seeds of problems for the next generation, particularly when, as is sometimes the case, the ex-prisoner becomes a "monster."

Jack B. Weinstein, Senior Judge, U.S. District Court, Eastern District of New York, Adjudicative Justice in a Diverse Mass Society, 8 J. L. & Pol'y 385, 410 (2000)

Classroom Exercise

Pair off with one other member of your class or study group. Each of you then write down on a piece of paper five propositions having to do with politics or social reality that you believe to be true, such as that women should have the right to choose whether to have an abortion, that everyone should be judged by the same standards for admission to school, or that the best government is one that governs least. You then offer a counterexample to one of the other person's propositions, for example, a case of governmental intervention that worked.

How did the other person react? Did he or she accept your argument and modify his or her position? What was the force of your "narrative," and why did it succeed or fail? Then, reverse places and consider your partner's case against one of your beliefs.

3. Serving Two Masters

Derrick Bell has pointed out a third structure that impedes reform, this time in law. To litigate a law-reform case, the lawyer needs a flesh-and-blood client. One might wish to establish the right of poor consumers to rescind a sales contract or to challenge the legal fiction that a school district is desegregated if the authorities have arranged that the makeup of certain schools is half black and half Chicano (as some of them did in the wake of *Brown v. Board of Education*).

Suppose, however, that the client and his or her community do not want the very same remedy that the lawyer does. The lawyer, who may represent a civil rights or public interest organization, may want a sweeping decree that names a new evil and declares it contrary to constitutional principles. He or she may be willing to gamble and risk all. The client, however, may want something different—better schools or more money for the ones in his or her neighborhood. He or she may want bilingual education or more black teachers, instead of classes taught by prize-winning white teachers with Ph.D.s. A lawyer representing a poor client may want to litigate the right to a welfare hearing, while the client may be more interested in a new pair of Sunday shoes for his or her child. These conflicts, which are ubiquitous in law-reform situations, haunt the lawyer pursuing social change and seem inherent in our system of legal remedies. Which master should the lawyer serve? Do similar conflicts arise in the political realm? For example, does a black president or senator, by the very nature of his or her role, have to downplay his or her blackness in fulfilling obligations to the country as a whole?

Classroom Exercise: Who Should Call the Shots?

Professor Hamar Aziz is a physicist of Egyptian descent who teaches at a major research university. Aziz recently attempted to fly to an international conference in Geneva but was turned aside at the local airport by TSA officials who told him that his name was on a no-fly list. Aziz, who missed an opportunity to present his latest paper, is furious and wants you to help redress the harm he has suffered and make sure that it does not happen again to him. In short, he wants the government to take his name off the list so that he can fly once again. Your research shows that the no-fly list is full of errors and results in the grounding of many innocent passengers, some of whom, like Aziz, merely happen to have the same name as someone who has attracted the attention of the authorities. Aziz is the perfect candidate to challenge the list, since he has a sparkling record, is a former Marine officer and Boy Scout troop leader, and was an alternate to the U.S. Olympic team in the long jump. Aziz, however, is mainly interested in getting himself off the list. Should you take his case?

4. Race Remedies Law as a Homeostatic Device

Some crits, such as Derrick Bell and Alan Freeman, even argue that our system of civil rights law and enforcement ensures that racial progress occurs at just the right slow pace. Too slow would make minorities impatient and risk destabilization; too fast could jeopardize important material and psychic benefits for elite groups. When the gap between our ideals and practices becomes too great, the system produces a "contradiction-closing case," so that everyone will think that it is truly fair and just. And on those rare occasions when social conditions call for a genuine concession, such as affirmative action, the costs of that concession are always placed on minorities—in the form of stigma—or on working-class whites, like Alan Bakke, who sought admission to the University of California at Davis Medical School, who are least able to incur them.

In her amended complaint, Monteiro alleged that her ninth-grade daughter and other similarly situated African-American students attended a school where they were called "niggers" by white children, and where that term was written on the walls of the buildings in which they were supposed to learn civics and social studies. It does not take an educational psychologist to conclude that being referred to by one's peers by the most noxious racial epithet in the contemporary American lexicon, being shamed and humiliated on the basis of one's race, and having the school authorities ignore or reject one's complaints would adversely affect a Black child's ability to obtain the same benefit from schooling as her white counterparts. . . . It is the beginning of high school, when a young adolescent is highly impressionable and is making decisions about education that will affect the course of her life. . . . [A] school where this sort of conduct occurs unchecked is utterly failing in its mandate to provide a nondiscriminatory educational environment. Accordingly, we find that the complaint sets forth allegations that satisfy the first factor of the test for a Title VI violation.

Monteiro v. Tempe Union High School District, 158 F.3d 1022, 1039 (9th Cir. 1998) (Before Monteiro, a nearly unbroken string of decisions rejected relief for minority plaintiffs subjected to racist slurs and struck down campus speech codes.)

QUESTIONS AND COMMENTS FOR CHAPTER II

1. If society agreed to think only kind thoughts about people of color, would their condition improve very much? How much, and in the short or the long run?

2. If society agreed to treat everyone, including people of color, exactly the same, would the condition of communities of color improve very much? Again, in the short or the long run?

3. If American Indians discovered gold on the reservation or blacks did the same in the inner city, so that the average wealth and family income of Indians and blacks were exactly the same as those of whites, would racism abate? Become more intense? Stay the same?

4. Today more African Americans attend segregated schools than they did when *Brown v. Board of Education* was decided. What does this say about reform through law?

5. Beginning with *Brown* and continuing through the sixties and early seventies, the Supreme Court handed down a number of decisions favorable to blacks and other minorities. Now it has been limiting affirmative action and weakening enforcement under antidiscrimination laws. What explains the shift?

6. Is society, over time, becoming more, or less, fair in its treatment of minorities? If your answer is "more fair," why are courts making it harder to vote? If your answer is "less fair," how do you account for Obama's presidency?

7. When is a favorable judicial decision a contradiction-closing case?

8. Suppose you are litigating an employment-discrimination case on behalf of a black woman who suffered ill treatment at work on account of her black womanhood. The employer points out that he does not discriminate against black men (and rather likes them) or against white women. Your suit, in short, requires that the law recognize a new cause of action for intersectional categories, such as black women, who are members of two groups at the same time. Do you suspect that legal research in a commercial database would unearth the few decisions that have adjudicated such claims? Suppose the category, as yet, lacks an agreed-upon name?

9. You are a social activist who has recently come to believe that Derrick Bell's interest-convergence hypothesis— that whites allow breakthroughs for blacks only when it serves whites' interests—makes sense. Will this change your approach to activism, and, if so, how?

SUGGESTED READINGS

Bell, Derrick A., Jr., Brown v. Board of Education and the Interest-Convergence Dilemma, 93 Harv. L. Rev. 518 (1980).

Bell, Derrick A., Jr., Serving Two Masters: Integration Ideals and Client Interests in School Desegregation Litigation, 85 Yale L.J. 470 (1976).

Bender, Steven, Mea Culpa: Lessons on Law and Regret from U.S. History (2015).

Coates, Ta-Nehisi, Between the World and Me (2015).

Crenshaw, Kimberlé W., Race, Reform, and Retrenchment: Transformation and Legitimation in Antidiscrimination Law, 101 Harv. L. Rev. 1331 (1988).

Delgado, Richard & Jean Stefancic, Why Do We Tell the Same Stories? Law Reform, Critical Librarianship, and the Triple Helix Dilemma, 42 Stan. L. Rev. 207 (1989).

Dudziak, Mary L., Cold War Civil Rights: Race and the Image of America Democracy (2000).

Dyson, Michael Eric, The Black Presidency: Barack Obama and the Politics of Race in America (2016).

Freeman, Alan D., Legitimizing Racial Discrimination through Antidiscrimination Law: A Critical Review of Supreme Court Doctrine, 62 Minn. L. Rev. 1049 (1978).

Gotanda, Neil, A Critique of "Our Constitution Is Color-Blind," 44 Stan. L. Rev. 1 (1991).

Guinier, Lani, Demosprudence through Dissent, 122 Harv. L. Rev. 4 (2008).

Haney López, Ian F., Dog Whistle Politics: How Coded Racial Appeals Have Reinvented Racism and Wrecked the Middle Class (2013).

Lawrence, Charles R., III, The Id, the Ego, and Equal Protection: Reckoning with Unconscious Racism, 39 Stan. L. Rev. 317 (1987).

Peller, Gary, Critical Race Consciousness: Reconsidering America's Ideologies of Racial Justice (2012).

Williams, Robert A., Like a Loaded Weapon: The Rehnquist Court, Indian Rights, and the Legal History of Racism in America (2005).

Zinn, Howard, A People's History of the United States: 1492–Present (20th Anniversary ed. 1999).

CHAPTER III

Legal Storytelling and Narrative Analysis

Have you ever had the experience of hearing one story and being completely convinced, then hearing an exactly opposite story, equally well told, and being left unsure of your convictions? In an everyday experience, Kim complains to the teacher that Billy has been picking fights on the playground. The teacher listens sympathetically and is ready to punish Billy. Fortunately, the teacher listens to Billy's story or that of an impartial third child. It turns out that Billy is not at fault at all; Kim started the trouble.

Or have you perhaps had the experience of watching two gifted appellate lawyers arguing a case? You hear the first and are persuaded. You see no way that the court can fail to rule in his or her favor. Then the second lawyer argues the opposite side, citing different authority, invoking different principles, bringing out different aspects of the same cases that the first lawyer relied on. Your certainty is shaken; now you are unsure which side deserves to win.

Or perhaps you have had the experience of discussing with a friend a famous case, such as the one growing out of the death of Trayvon Martin or one having to do with an accused terrorist who was tortured. You and she agree

*on most of the facts of what happened, but you put radi-
cally different interpretations on them. You are left won-
dering how two people can see "the same evidence" in
such different lights.*

Critical race theorists have built on everyday experiences with perspective, viewpoint, and the power of stories
and persuasion to come to a deeper understanding of how
Americans see race. They have written parables, autobiog-
raphy, and "counterstories" and have investigated the fac-
tual background and personalities, frequently ignored in
the casebooks, of well-known cases such as *Korematsu*
(the Japanese-internment case) or *Plessy v. Ferguson* (the
separate-but-equal case). Other scholars have examined
narrative theory in an effort to understand why certain
stories work and others do not. Still others study the
way trial lawyers consciously or unconsciously construct
narratives—theories of a case—that they hope will resonate
with the jury and induce it to adopt their interpretations
of what happened and to reject those of the opposite side.

Legal storytellers, such as Derrick Bell and Patricia Williams, draw on a long history with roots going back to the
slave narratives, tales written by black captives to describe
their condition and unmask the gentility that white plantation society pretended to. American Indians, of course,
were great storytellers who used history and myth to pre-
serve culture, to bind the group together, and to remind it
of its common destiny. In Latino society, picaresque novel-
ists made sly fun of social convention, puffed-up nobility,
and illegitimate authority. Although some writers criticize

CRT for excessive negativity and failure to develop a positive program, legal storytelling and narrative analysis are clear-cut advances that the movement can claim. Even some minority judges are finding it useful from time to time to insist on the validity of the perspective of color.

> By that standard, white judges will be permitted to keep the latitude they have enjoyed for centuries in discussing matters of intellectual substance, even issues of human rights and, because they are white, still be permitted to later decide specific factual situations involving the principles of human rights which they have discussed previously in a generalized fashion. But for black judges, defendants insist on a far more rigid standard, which would preclude black judges from ever discussing race relations even in . . . generalized fashion. . . .
>
> To suggest that black judges should be so disqualified would be analogous to suggesting that the slave masters were right when . . . they argued that only they, but not the slaves, could evaluate the harshness or justness of the system.
>
> *Federal Judge Leon Higginbotham, in refusing to disqualify himself from hearing a case, Commonwealth v. Local Union 542, International Union of Operating Engineers, 388 F. Supp. 155 , 165 (E.D. Pa. 1974)*

A. Opening a Window onto Ignored or Alternative Realities

One premise of legal storytellers is that members of this country's dominant racial group cannot easily grasp what it is like to be nonwhite. Few have what W. E. B. Du Bois described as "double consciousness." History books, Sunday sermons, and even case law contribute to a cultural hegemony that makes it difficult for reformers to make race an issue. How to bridge the gap in thinking between persons of good will whose experiences, perspectives, and backgrounds are radically different is a great challenge.

Consider the following clash of stories. According to one leading CRT writer, the majority's story of race would probably go something like this:

Early in our history there was slavery, which was a terrible thing. Blacks were brought to this country from Africa in chains and made to work in the fields. Some were viciously mistreated, which was, of course, an unforgivable wrong; others were treated kindly. Slavery ended with the Civil War, although many blacks remained poor, uneducated, and outside the cultural mainstream. As the country's racial sensitivity to blacks' plight increased, federal statutes and case law gradually eliminated the vestiges of slavery. Today, blacks enjoy many civil rights and are protected from discrimination in such areas as housing, public education, employment, and voting. A black president occupies the White House. Many entertainers and sports figures—millionaires all—are black. The gap between blacks and whites is steadily closing, although it may take some time for it to close completely. At the same time, it is important not to go too far in providing special benefits for blacks. Doing so induces dependency and welfare mentality. It can also cause a backlash among innocent whites who believe they have suffered reverse discrimination. Most Americans are fair-minded individuals who harbor little racial prejudice. The few who do can be punished when they act on those beliefs.

That's the first story. Yet coexisting with that comforting tale are others of black, Chinese, Japanese, Latino, Filipino, and American Indian subordination in the United States, a history "gory, brutal, filled with more murder, mutilation, rape, and brutality than most of us can imagine or easily comprehend" (Derrick Bell, And We Are Not Saved 217 [1987]).

That history continues into the present and implicates persons still alive. It includes infant death rates among minorities nearly double those of whites, as well as arrest and incarceration rates that are among the highest in the world. School dropout rates among blacks and Latinos are worse than those in practically any industrialized country, and the gap between whites and nonwhites in income, assets, educational attainment, and life expectancy is as wide as it was thirty years ago, if not wider. Violence against Middle Eastern–looking people, as well as against sexual minorities, has increased alarmingly.

The new accounts dare to call our most prized legal doctrines and protections shams—hollow pronouncements issued with great solemnity and fanfare, only to be silently ignored, cut back, or withdrawn when the celebrations die down.

How can there be such divergent stories? Why do they not reconcile? To the first question, critical race theory answers, "experience." People of different races have radically different experiences as they go through life. (Derrick Bell would add a further reason: "interest convergence"— people believe what benefits them.) To the second, it answers that empathy is in short supply. (See the discussion of the empathic fallacy in chapter 2.) Literary and narrative theory holds that we each occupy a normative universe or "nomos" (or perhaps many of them), from which we are not easily dislodged. Talented storytellers nevertheless struggle to reach broad audiences with their messages. "Everyone loves a story." The hope is that well-told stories describing the reality of black and brown lives can help readers to bridge the gap between their worlds and those of others. Engaging stories can help us understand what life is like for others and invite the reader into a new and unfamiliar world.

"Race may be America's single most confounding problem, but the confounding problem of race is that few people seem to know what race is." (Ian F. Haney López, The Social Construction of Race: Some Observations on Illusion, Fabrication, and Choice, 29 Harv. C.R.-C.L. L. Rev. 1, 5–6 [1994]). In part, what makes race a confounding problem and what causes many people to not know what race is, is the view that the problems of race are the problems of the racial minority. They are not. The problems of race belong to all of us, no matter where our ancestors come from, no matter what the color of our skin. Thus, concluding that race is not an issue in this case because juror 32 is not a member of a racial minority, misses the point. Race is an issue.

State v. Buggs, 581 N.W. 2d 329, 344 (Minn. 1998)

B. Counterstorytelling

Some of the critical storytellers believe that stories also have a valid destructive function. Society constructs the social world through a series of tacit agreements mediated by images, pictures, tales, tweets, blog postings, social media, and other scripts. Much of what we believe is ridiculous, self-serving, or cruel but is not perceived to be so at the time. Attacking embedded preconceptions that marginalize others or conceal their humanity is a legitimate function of all fiction.

In legal discourse, preconceptions and myths, for example, about black criminality or Muslim terrorism, shape mindset—the bundle of received wisdoms, stock stories, and suppositions that allocate suspicion, place the burden of proof on one party or the other, and tell us in cases of divided evidence what probably happened. These cultural influences are probably at least as determinative of outcomes as are the formal laws, since they supply the background against which the latter are interpreted and applied. Critical writers use counterstories to challenge, displace, or mock these pernicious narratives and beliefs. (See, e.g., Richard Delgado, Rodrigo's Eighth Chronicle: Black Crime, White Fears—On the Social Construction of Threat, 80 Va. L. Rev. 503 [1994], pointing out that white-collar and corporate/industrial crime—perpetrated mostly by whites—causes more personal injury, death, and property loss than does all street crime combined, even on a per capita basis.)

C. Cure for Silencing

Stories also serve a powerful additional function for minority communities. Many victims of racial discrimination suffer in silence or blame themselves for their predicament. Others pretend that it didn't happen or that they "just let it roll off my back." All three groups are more silent than they need be. Stories can give them a voice and reveal that other people have similar experiences. Stories can name a type of discrimination (e.g., microaggressions, unconscious discrimination, or structural racism); once named, it can be combated. If race is not real or objective but constructed, racism and prejudice should be capable of deconstruction; the pernicious beliefs and categories are, after all, our own. Powerfully written stories and narratives may begin a process of correction in our system of beliefs and categories by calling attention to neglected evidence and reminding readers of our common humanity. Even the conservative judge Richard Posner has conceded that major reforms in law often come through a conversion process or paradigm shift similar to the one Thomas Kuhn describes and minority storytellers advocate (Richard Posner, The Problems of Jurisprudence 459 [1990]). Barack Obama's *Dreams from My Father* (1995) seems to have served a vital function in explaining to many readers the young president's racial journey.

The philosopher Jean-François Lyotard's concept of the *differend* helps explain the value of narratives for marginalized persons. The differend occurs when a concept such as justice acquires conflicting meanings for two groups. A prime example would be a case in which a judge seeks to hold responsible an individual who does not subscribe to the foundational views of the regime that is sitting in judgment of him or her. In situations like this, the subordinate person lacks language to express how he or she has been injured or wronged. (See, e.g., George Martinez,

Philosophical Considerations and the Use of Narrative in the Law, 30 Rutgers L.J. 683 [1999].) For example, when contemporary Euro-Americans resist even discussing reparations for blacks on the grounds that a black person living today has never been a slave and so lacks standing, nor has any white person alive today been a slaveholder, the black person who wishes to discuss these questions and is shunted aside suffers the differend. The prevailing conception of justice deprives him or her of the chance to express a grievance in terms the system will understand. Until very recently, women who suffered childhood incest or battered-wife syndrome were victims of the differend, as were Latino undocumented persons who suffered workplace discrimination but could not complain for fear of being deported. Narratives provide a language to bridge the gaps in imagination and conception that give rise to the differend. They reduce alienation for members of excluded groups, while offering opportunities for members of the majority group to meet them halfway. In our time, Middle Eastern writers describe the alienation and pain of dealing with daily suspicion that they are terrorists, when they may be law-abiding accountants, teachers, office workers, or doctors. (See, e.g., John Tehranian, Whitewashed: America's Invisible Middle Eastern Minority [2008].)

D. Storytelling in Court

Attorneys and teachers of clinical law have been applying storytelling and narrative analysis to understand how the dynamics of persuasion operate in the courtroom. They also use them to understand the interplay of power and interpretive authority between lawyer and client. Suppose, for example, the lawyer favors strategy A because it is 60 percent likely to win. The client, however, favors strategy B because it is "truer" to his experience or his world, even though it is less likely to produce a victory. Writers such as Lucy White and Anthony Alfieri show that attention to the narrative side of lawyering can enable lawyers representing the poor and disenfranchised to achieve a better brand of justice. This has prompted some critics to charge that CRT teaches unmitigated manipulation of emotions and playing the race card. For example, when the O. J. Simpson verdict came down, Jeffrey Rosen, legal affairs writer for the *New Republic*, charged that Johnny Cochran's successful defense of his famous client was an outrage and a case of "applied critical race theory." Despite this and other criticisms, law has been slowly moving in the direction of recognizing the legitimacy and power of narrative. Children and certain other witnesses are permitted to testify in the form of an uninterrupted narrative, rather than through question-and-answer examination. With sexual-offense victims, shield laws and evidentiary statutes protect them against certain types of examination, even though the Sixth Amendment's Confrontation Clause would otherwise permit the other side to attack their narrative forcefully.

E. Storytelling on the Defensive

Storytelling, as exemplified by the best-selling books of Derrick Bell, Patricia Williams, and others, has enjoyed a considerable vogue that has spread to other disciplines. It should not be a surprise, then, that the legal storytelling movement has come in for sharp criticism. Some of it comes from conservatives, like federal judge Richard Posner, who disagree, substantively, with what the crits are saying. But criticism also comes from leftist scholars, like Mark Tushnet, who consider that the genre is an ineffective and analytically unsound form of discourse, and from self-professed liberals, like Daniel Farber and Suzanna Sherry, whose critiques are discussed in chapter 6.

QUESTIONS AND COMMENTS FOR CHAPTER III

1. Why are most legal storytellers black or brown (Derrick Bell, Richard Delgado, Patricia Williams, Tara Yosso, Matthew Fletcher, Mari Matsuda, etc.)?

2. Do white people tell stories, too, but deem them not stories at all but the truth?

3. If one wanted to change another person's mind about something, say, the death penalty, what would be more effective, an array of statistics or a good story or movie?

4. "Once upon a time . . ." Do stories (at least ones that are well told) cause the reader or listener to suspend disbelief, and, if so, is this a good or a bad thing?

5. Suppose you have a particular account of the world. For example, as a result of experience you have come to believe that virtue is almost always rewarded and that people generally get what they deserve. Social handouts and welfare just make matters worse. Someone tells you a story about a welfare recipient who used her allotment to raise her children, then went to school and became a Ph.D. and owner of a start-up computer company. How do you react? Do you reconsider your views—or merely pronounce her an exception?

6. What stories do you tend to hear in the debate over affirmative action? Which ones do you hear over and over again during presidential campaigns? (Self-made man? Patriotic American? Tells it like it is? Defender of the Constitution?) During judicial confirmation hearings? (Will stick to the rule of law? Future judicial activist? Understands the common man?)

7. Is capitalism—our society's dominant mode of doing business—a collection of stories, for example, that the market is the best way of allocating resources, that if everyone pursues his or her own self-interest, society will benefit from the citizenry's energy and inventions, and that state control is almost always bad? If it is, will capitalism's periodic crises and crashes eventually cause its supporters to modify their views? Or are stories of this kind impervious to experience?

8. If you hear a given story too often, does a discrepant item of evidence merely cause you to ignore it?

9. Suppose you have a friend who believes in a militarized border and strict enforcement of immigration laws. During a discussion, you learn that she believes that immigration brings Mexican criminals and terrorists into the country and increases the chances of the "next 9/11." You have read studies showing that regions that have experienced increased immigration, including the undocumented kind, see decreasing (not increasing) crime rates. You have also read that to date not a single foreign terrorist is known to have sneaked across the border from Mexico. Are studies like these likely to persuade her to change her views on immigration, and, if not, why not?

10. How can a community activist employ storytelling in his or her work?

SUGGESTED READINGS

Alfieri, Anthony V., Resistance Songs: Mobilizing the Law and Politics of Community, 93 Texas L. Rev. 1459 (2015).

Amsterdam, Anthony G. & Jerome Bruner, Minding the Law: How Courts Rely on Storytelling and How Their Stories Change the Ways We Understand the Law—and Ourselves (2001).

Bell, Derrick A., Jr., And We Are Not Saved: The Elusive Quest for Racial Justice (1987).

Delgado, Richard, Storytelling for Oppositionists and Others: A Plea for Narrative, 87 Mich. L. Rev. 2411 (1989).

Law Stories Series (West Pub. Co.).

Martinez, George A., Race, American Law, and the State of Nature, 112 W. Va. L. Rev. 799 (2010).

Matsuda, Mari J., Looking to the Bottom: Critical Legal Studies and Reparations, 22 Harv. C.R.-C.L. L. Rev. 323 (1987).

Symposium: Legal Storytelling, 87 Mich. L. Rev. 2073 (1989).

Troutt, David D., The Monkey Suit and Other Short Fiction on African Americans and Justice (1998).

White, Lucie E., Subordination, Rhetorical Survival Skills, and Sunday Shoes: Notes on the Hearing of Mrs. G., 38 Buff. L. Rev. 1 (1990).

Williams, Patricia J., The Alchemy of Race and Rights: Diary of a Law Professor (1991).

Yosso, Tara J., Critical Race Counterstories along the Chicana/o Educational Pipeline (2006).

CHAPTER IV

Looking Inward

Because politics has a personal dimension, it should come as no surprise that critical race theorists have turned critique inward, examining the interplay of power and authority within minority communities, movements, and even selves. This chapter analyzes several aspects of that interplay—intersectionality; antiessentialism; the tensions between nationalism and assimilation; and racial mixture and identity.

A. *Intersectionality*

"Intersectionality" means the examination of race, sex, class, national origin, and sexual orientation and how their combination plays out in various settings. These categories—and still others—can be separate disadvantaging factors. What happens when an individual occupies more than one of these categories, for example, is both gay and Native American or both female and black? Individuals like these operate at an intersection of recognized sites of oppression. Do such cases require that each disadvantaging factor be considered separately, additively, or in yet some other fashion? Should persons who experience multiple forms of oppression have their own categories and representation, apart from those that correspond to the separate varieties of discrimination they experience? And what about the role of these "intersectional" persons in social movements such as feminism or gay liberation? Where do they belong? These are all questions that intersectional analysis attempts to address.

Imagine a black woman. She may be oppressed because of her race. She may also be so because of her gender. If she is a single working mother, she may experience discrimination by virtue of that status as well. She experiences, potentially, not only multiple forms of oppression but ones unique to her and to others like her. Suppose that such a person experiences discrimination at her workplace. She arrives one day to find a new supervisor, who, it turns out, does not like black women, believing them lazy and unreliable. He also thinks that many of them have an "attitude problem." So he assigns her disagreeable work, requires her to notify him whenever she leaves her work area, and neglects to advise her of opportunities for promotion for which she is otherwise qualified.

She resolves to sue. But on what theory? Suppose she sues for racial discrimination—her supervisor does discriminate against her because she is black. But suppose it turns out that the supervisor does not dislike black men and, in fact, treats them well. He likes playing basketball with them after work, discussing sports with them on Monday, and engaging in easy banter with them about music or popular entertainment. Under current law, the supervisor might well successfully defend against a discrimination suit, since he does not discriminate against blacks per se—just against black women.

Suppose, then, that she resolves to sue for sex discrimination. She is, after all, a black woman, and her supervisor does discriminate against her because of her sex. Once again, however, she might easily lose. The supervisor might show that he is not biased against women as a class and, indeed, enjoys having white women working for him. He finds white women attractive and good, reliable workers. He even occasionally dates one. White women remind him of his sister. He finds the younger ones pretty and decorative. He likes having them around.

Our plaintiff, then, will probably be unable to prove discrimination based on either race or sex. Yet she suffers discrimination based on her black womanhood. This is one aspect of the intersectional dilemma.

She may face a similar predicament in ordinary politics. Imagine that she wants to join with others in a movement to change society's treatment of people like her. She might look to the feminist movement for support and solidarity. But she is likely to find that this white-dominated movement embraces an agenda and a set of concerns that arise out of the white female experience, for example, the glass ceiling, abortion rights, and the election of a female president of the United States. She is more interested in day-care reform and Head Start programs for her young children. She may also be interested in protection from domestic abuse at the hands of black men. The feminist movement welcomes her with open arms, for she is one *more soldier to add to the ranks. But will its agenda ever get around to addressing her concerns?*

Imagine, then, that she resolves to join the civil rights movement, hoping to address the type of discrimination that she suffers at work. This time she finds that racism is indeed the primary focus of the group. It supports affirmative action, restructuring the criminal justice system to eradicate racial disparities, and electing black mayors. It supports measures to end racial profiling and highway stops for "driving while black." But while these concerns are ones she shares as a black person, they are not necessarily the ones at the top of her agenda. The male-dominated civil rights movement will welcome her and persons like her, needing their numbers, but until women become a significant force within the group, it is apt to afford her concerns scant attention. Movement leaders may even ask her to stuff envelopes, run errands, answer the telephone, or make coffee.

If she persists in raising her concerns, she may even find herself accused of being divisive. Feminists may tell her to put aside her concerns as a black woman for a moment, in the interest of a "united" sisterhood, while the black men may be so caught up with life-and-death issues, such as disproportionate imposition of the death penalty or Tasering of black male motorists who do not respond quickly enough to police commands, that they react impatiently to her requests to consider her predicament at work.

When movements for racial justice prioritize broad concerns over those of particular subgroups, many needs, such as those of our hypothetical black woman, may go unaddressed. This is no small problem. Many races are divided along lines of socioeconomic status, politics, religion, sexual orientation, and national origin, each of which generates intersectional individuals. Even within groups that are seemingly homogeneous, one finds attitudinal differences. Consider, for example, responses to black criminality. Some members of the black community hold that not enough of society's attention goes to law-abiding black citizens who are the victims of crime in black neighborhoods. This get-tough viewpoint is an example of what has been called a "politics of respectability" and disavows any identification with black criminality. It wants more, not fewer, police and harsher, not softer, sentences for black offenders. The opposite perspective within the black community is sometimes called the "politics of identification." Persons of this persuasion identify with the "race rebel" aspect of some black criminals and support them, at least if they are young, redeemable, and a potential asset to the community. African Americans who hold this view want the police to leave certain black offenders alone and let the community handle them. Antisnitching campaigns in black neighborhoods are evidence of this attitude. (Some Latino groups do something similar when they shelter or aid undocumented immigrants.)

Categories and subgroups, then, are not just matters of theoretical interest. How we frame them determines who has power, voice, and representation and who does not. Perspectivalism, the insistence on examining how things look from the perspective of individual actors, helps us understand the predicament of intersectional individuals. It can enable us to frame approaches that may do justice to a broad range of people and avoid oversimplifying human experience.

A related critical tool that has proven useful in this respect is the notion of multiple consciousness, which holds that most of us experience the world in different ways on different occasions, because of who we are. The hope is that if we pay attention to the multiplicity of social life, perhaps our institutions and arrangements will better address the problems that plague us. The growing number of multiracial individuals suggests that this concern will only increase.

B. Essentialism and Antiessentialism

Do all oppressed people have something in common? This question lies at the heart of the essentialism/antiessentialism debate. On one level, the answer is obvious: of course all oppressed people have something in common—their oppression. But the forms of that oppression may vary from group to group. And if they do, the needs and political strategies of groups fighting for social change will vary as well. When a group organizes for social change, it must have a clear concept of what it is fighting to achieve. Essentialism, then, entails a search for the proper unit, or atom, of social analysis and change.

When we think of the term "essentializing," we think of paring something down until the heart of the matter stands alone. Essentialism has a political dimension. As mentioned in the previous section, the goals of a "unified" group may not reflect exactly those of certain factions within it, yet the larger group benefits from their participation because of the increased numbers they bring. We saw this in the case of the single black mother who sought to identify with a social movement but was thwarted on finding that the priorities of the two groups most likely to welcome her did not correspond to her life experience.

This tension seems inherent in our mode of existence. Large numbers of people motivated for social change have the power to alter social practice and perception. This is evident in the early achievements of the women's and civil rights movements. Today, hardly anyone expresses the view publicly that "women shouldn't work outside the home" or "people of color are intellectually inferior to whites." Would these advances in public consciousness have come about if underrepresented subgroups, such as black women, gay men, or Latino and Asian American Ph.D.s, had decided to sit things out?

It takes a multitude of the oppressed to make their voices heard and felt. But what about the voices that do not fit into one single category of oppression? Will social progress let them slip through the cracks? These issues are particularly acute regarding inter- and intraminority relations and tensions (see chapter 5). They also explain some of the crits' impatience with liberalism. The reader will recall that CRT takes liberalism to task for its cautious, incremental quality (see chapter 2). When we are tackling a structure as deeply embedded as race, radical measures are in order—otherwise the system merely swallows up the small improvement one has made, and everything goes back to the way it was.

Ignoring the problem of intersectionality, as liberalism often does, risks doing things by half measures and leaving major sectors of the population dissatisfied. Classical liberalism also has been criticized as overly caught up in the search for universals, such as admissions standards for universities or sentencing guidelines that are the same for all. The crits point out that this approach is apt to do injustice to individuals whose experience and situation differ from the norm. They call for individualized treatment—"context"—that pays attention to minorities' lives. This deficiency is apt to be particularly glaring in the case of "double minorities," such as black women, gay Latinos, or Muslim women wearing head scarves, whose lives are twice removed from the experience of mainstream Americans.

Some observers hold that all minority races should compromise their differences and form a united front against racism in general. The danger in this essentialized approach is that certain minority groups, socioeconomic classes, and sexual orientations may end up better off and others worse. Recall how shabbily black women were treated in the civil rights movement of the 1960s, rarely allowed to speak for the group, made to march in the second row, and relegated, with a few exceptions, to support roles. Only lately have black women and Latinas emerged as powerful voices on the American scene. Perhaps the essentialism/antiessentialism debate sets in when mainstream thought is beginning to see the validity in the larger groups' complaints. Like an automobile with deferred maintenance, smaller subgroups that have until then remained silent begin bringing suppressed issues to the larger group's attention. And so the dialectic continues.

C. Nationalism versus Assimilation

Two friends, William and Jamal, are walking down a main street. Both are African Americans and have been close friends since high school. Both have medium-brown skin and hazel eyes. Both are graduates of prestigious universities. William wears a business suit and carries a briefcase made by a famous designer. He is a third-year associate at a large law firm. Jamal, who is a music-industry executive making twice as much money as William, is sporting a tasteful kente shirt and wearing his hair in corn rows. On their way to a lunch date to discuss a new recording contract, they talk about mutual friends, their families, and their careers. On arriving at the restaurant, a trendy downtown eating establishment that caters to young professionals, William and Jamal exchange looks, and without speaking William enters first and asks the maitre d' for a quiet table for two.

The two friends illustrate twin poles in the way minorities of color can represent and position themselves. The nationalist, or separatist, position illustrated by Jamal holds that people of color should embrace their culture and origins. Jamal, who by choice lives in an upscale black neighborhood and sends his children to local schools, could easily fit into mainstream life. But he feels more comfortable working and living in black milieux and considers that he has a duty to contribute to the minority community. Accordingly, he does as much business as possible with other blacks. The last time he and his family moved, for example, he made several phone calls until he found a black-owned moving company. He donates money to several African American philanthropies and colleges. And, of course, his work in the music industry allows him the opportunity to boost the careers of black musicians, which he does.

William also donates to several black causes. And, although he practices law in a white-dominated law firm on behalf of corporate clients, most of whom are white, he does pro bono work whenever possible on behalf of prison inmates, a large majority of whom are African American. He lives in an integrated suburb that is 90 percent white with a smattering of blacks and other people of color, most professionals like himself.

William and Jamal have discussed their contrasting lifestyles and have agreed to disagree. William believes he is doing more good breaking barriers in the white-dominated legal world and that his work as a lawyer, especially when he is crowned with the partnership he expects in a few years, will enable him to do some real good on behalf of minority clients and businesses. And even though Jamal is currently making more money than he, William believes that his own top salary as a partner will one day match that of his high school friend.

Debates about nationalism versus assimilation figure prominently in current discourse about race. One strand of critical race theory energetically backs the nationalist view, which is particularly prominent with the materialists. Derrick Bell, for example, urged his fellow African Americans to foreswear the struggle for school integration and aim for building the best possible black schools. Other CRT nationalists advocate gun ownership, on the grounds that historically the police in this country have not protected blacks against violence, indeed have often visited it upon them. Other nationalists urge the establishment of all-black inner-city schools, sometimes just for males, on the grounds that boys of color need strong role models and cannot easily find them in the public schools. Others back black- or Latino-run charter schools in big cities. Nationalists of all types question the majoritarian assumption that northern European culture is superior. Most support ethnic studies departments at the university level.

At the high school level, a Latino studies program in at least one district (Tucson, Arizona) drew the ire of state officials, who enacted a ban on any program that teaches ethnic division. The program's supporters, of course, pointed out that they were merely teaching students their own history and pride in their own culture. They also emphasized that the program was not closed to non-Latino students and was very popular. When local authorities gave in to state officials' threat to cut the district's funding and eliminated the program, the community exploded in outrage. Their indignation increased when school officials removed the program's texts, which included William Shakespeare's *The Tempest*, Paolo Freire's *Pedagogy of the Oppressed*, and the very book you are reading, from the shelves of the classrooms, in front of crying students. In response, the program's defenders staged protests, marched on the capital, and filed suit in federal court. A community-college instructor in Houston organized an automobile caravan hauling trunks full of "wet books" on the banned list all the way to Tucson, where the drivers gave them away to students and passersby on the sidewalks of that city.

Latino nationalists also endorse preservation of the Spanish language and ties with Mexico, Puerto Rico, and the Caribbean or other homelands. A few speak of restoring what is now the U.S. Southwest to something like its previous condition—the mythical land of Aztlán.

Both Latino and black nationalists take a dim view of passing—the effort to deracinate oneself and present oneself as white. Latino nationalists usually reject the term "Hispanic" because of its association with Spain, the nation that oppressed their ancestors in Mexico and Central and South America. Nationalists honor ethnic studies and history as vital disciplines and look with skepticism on members of their groups who date, marry, or form close friendships with whites or seek employment in white-dominated workplaces or industries. Many Latino nationalists are sympathetic to Rodolfo Acuña's notion that Latinos in this country are an internal colony and that they should exploit that colonial status to build solidarity and resistance. Nationalists are apt to describe themselves as a nation within a nation and to hold that the loyalty and identification of black people, for example, should lie with that community and only secondarily with the United States.

A middle position, embraced by a few sophisticated thinkers, including on occasion Derrick Bell, holds that minorities of color should not try to fit into a flawed economic and political system but transform it. In this view, success, symbolized by a high income, token representation, and even a degree of influence, like that which William hopes to achieve, is not worth pursuing if the system itself remains unworthy and unjust.

A moderate position that falls between William's and Jamal's holds that it is acceptable for minorities to seek places in professions such as law, medicine, and business, so long as they apply their skills for the benefit of minority communities. In this view, nothing would be wrong with William's achievement of an Ivy League degree and bar certificate. But his practice in a corporate penthouse would be problematic; he should be a criminal or legal services lawyer instead. Or, if business law is his metier, then, like Jamal, he should be making his skills available to start-up black businesses.

A final intermediate position, one favoring William, holds that a strong U.S. economy benefits everyone. William's success as a black corporate lawyer produces wealth, some of which will trickle down to poor and minority communities; and, in any event, those communities need examples of successful, confident lawyers like William who can make their way anywhere.

Classroom Exercise

Divide your class or study group into two or more groups according to the aforementioned positions (Jamal's and William's). Each confers for ten minutes, selects spokespersons, and then argues the opposite position from the one they really believe.

D. Racial Mixture

Imagine that Jamal and William have a third friend, Rebecca, the daughter of a black father who is a school principal and a mother who is a Lebanese immigrant and a simultaneous translator for a large international agency. Rebecca, whose skin is medium brown, wears her hair in a short Afro and grew up in an upper-class suburb, where she attended highly competitive public schools. In college, she was a member of both the black student caucus (where she met Jamal and William), as well as the international student organization, which she joined in order to meet Middle Eastern people like her mother and practice her Arabic. She is currently a third-year medical student whose dream job is to be a physician with Doctors Without Borders, practicing medicine in far-flung areas of the developing world. She and Jamal have had several intense conversations about the medical needs of impoverished black communities in the United States. Jamal wishes she would devote herself to the needs of domestic people of color. William, who is ambivalent on this issue, is sitting out this discussion.

The number of mixed-race individuals in the United States is growing, as is the number of marriages among members of different minority groups. (See Kenneth Prewitt, Fix the Census' Archaic Racial Categories, N.Y. Times, Aug. 21, 2013.) Some mixed-race people have been asking for a category of their own in the U.S. Census and other official classification systems. Otherwise, some feel, they would be forced to disidentify with one side of their family or another. If Rebecca, who could be taken for black, lists herself that way and selects black friends as her main peer group, would she not, in effect, be rejecting her mother and her own Middle Eastern parentage?

QUESTIONS AND COMMENTS FOR CHAPTER IV

1. An Asian woman has been raising her hand at a meeting of white feminists planning a march to protest the "glass ceiling" in corporate management positions. When they finally recognize her, it turns out she wants to know when the group will discuss oppressive labor conditions in the garment industry. Is she being divisive?

2. Suppose the group responds that the agenda should reflect only items that concern all women "as women" and not ones that have to do with small factions, such as seamstresses in the clothing industry. Is the group implicitly adopting a middle-class white agenda?

3. Should minorities make an effort to "fit in" in social and work situations? Why or why not? Wouldn't this just be a lot of extra work?

4. If blacks or Chicanos sit at separate tables in the cafeteria, is that self-segregation? Should whites politely ask if they can join them?

5. Should minorities make an effort to do business with minority firms? Assume that Firm A and Firm B offer the same product or service, but one is run by Mr. Gonzalez and the other by a person whose ancestors came over on the *Mayflower*. Which one should the person of color patronize?

6. A politician is born in the United States to a white mother and a black father from Kenya. His parents separate while he is young, and he is raised, first, by his mother and then, when she dies, by his white grandparents, who send him to elite schools. He speaks unaccented English,

wears impeccable clothing, and exercises every day. Is he white, black, or neither?

7. Can a white person ever pass as black? Why would he? (See chapter 5.)

8. Can an assimilated minority-group member work within the system to bring about reform in a way that a rebellious outsider cannot?

9. Consider Devon Carbado and Mitu Gulati's notion of performative identity in the workplace, as well as Kenji Yoshino's concept of "covering," in which gays and lesbians work hard to conceal their identity from others. In performative identity, according to Carbado and Gulati, some workers of color carry the heavy burden of reassuring their coworkers on a daily basis that they are not threatening, uncouth, incompetent, and jivey. They do all this, of course, in addition to their assigned work, a type of double duty not expected from others. Should minorities indignantly refuse to do this, and what if it endangers their standing at work?

SUGGESTED READINGS

Acuña, Rodolfo, Occupied America (7th ed. 2010).

Austin, Regina, "The Black Community," Its Lawbreakers, and a Politics of Identification, 65 S. Cal. L. Rev. 1769 (1992).

Carbado, Devon, & Mitu Gulati, Working Identity, 85 Cornell L. Rev. 1259 (2000).

Collins, Patricia Hill, Black Sexual Politics: African Americans, Gender, and the New Racism (2005).

Crenshaw, Kimberlé W., Demarginalizing the Intersection of Race and Sex: A Black Feminist Critique of Antidiscrimination Doctrine, Feminist Theory, and Antiracist Politics, 1989 U. Chi. Legal F. 139.

Critical Race Feminism: A Reader (Adrien K. Wing ed., 2d ed. 2003).

Delgado, Richard, Rodrigo's Reconsideration: Intersectionality and the Future of Critical Race Theory, 96 Iowa L. Rev. 1247 (2011).

Harpalani, Vinay, Desicrit: Theorizing the Racial Ambiguity of South Asian Americans, 67 N.Y.U. Ann. Surv. Am. L. 77 (2013).

Harris, Angela P., Race and Essentialism in Feminist Legal Theory, 42 Stan. L. Rev. 581 (1990).

MacKinnon, Catharine A., From Practice to Theory, or What Is a White Woman, Anyway?, 4 Yale J.L. & Feminism 13 (1991).

Mixed-Race America and the Law: A Reader (Kevin R. Johnson ed., 2003).

Nunn, Kenneth B., Law as a Eurocentric Enterprise, 15 Law & Ineq. J. 323 (1997).

Onwuachi-Willig, Angela, A House Divided: The Invisibility of the Multiracial Family, 44 Harv. C.R.-C.L. L. Rev. 231 (2009).

Yancy, George, Who Is White? Latinos, Asians, and the New Black/Nonblack Divide (2003).

Yoshino, Kenji, Covering: The Hidden Assault on Our Civil Rights (2007).

CHAPTER V

Power and the Shape of Knowledge

Building on the previous chapter, we now consider further issues dealing with categories and power. Chapter 4 concerned the role of small subgroups within civil rights communities. This chapter addresses how we think about race and identity—the black-white binary, critical white studies, and Asian and Latino critical thought. Some of these issues are explosive, controversial, even divisive.

A. *The Black-White Binary*

One of the more contentious issues in American racial thought today is whether the very framework we use to consider problems of race reflects an unstated binary paradigm or mindset. That paradigm, the black-white binary, effectively dictates that nonblack minority groups must compare their treatment to that of African Americans to redress their grievances. The paradigm holds that one group, blacks, constitutes the prototypical minority group. "Race" means, quintessentially, African American. Others, such as Asians, American Indians, and Latinos, are minorities only insofar as their experience and treatment can be analogized to those of blacks.

Imagine, for example, that Juan Dominguez, a Puerto Rican worker, is told by his boss, "You're a lazy Puerto Rican just like all the rest. You'll never get ahead as long as I'm supervisor." Juan sues for workplace discrimination under a civil-rights-era statute designed, as most are, with blacks in mind. He wins because he can show that an African American worker, treated in similar fashion, would be entitled to redress. But suppose that Juan's coworkers and supervisor make fun of him because of his accent, religion, or place of birth. African Americans generally do not suffer discrimination on these grounds, so Juan would likely go without recourse.

The black-white binary is said to operate in everyday culture as well. Imagine that a group of liberal television executives says to each other, "Let's have a minority sitcom." The group is well meaning, but their thoughts are apt to go to a program whose central characters are a black family. Later, on second thought, they might add an Asian maid or a Latino teenager who is a friend of one of the family's children. But the essential framework for the program is likely to revolve around African American problems, in-jokes, and situations. Similarly, history textbooks may devote considerable space to the tremendously significant issue of slavery but overlook or devote scant treatment to the intense persecution of Chinese in California and elsewhere. Many may also ignore the equally important role of Conquest and the wars with Mexico and Spain in shaping Latino history. Even rarer would be a textbook that discusses the recent wave of intense anti-

Muslim suspicion that gripped the country in the years following 9/11.

A closely related concept is that of black, or any other kind of, exceptionalism. Exceptionalism holds that a group's history is so distinctive that placing it at the center of analysis is, in fact, warranted. For example, when a recent president convened a group of scholars and activists to lead a yearlong national conversation on race, at its first meeting, the chair, an eminent African American historian, proposed that the group "for the sake of simplicity" limit its consideration to African Americans. When other members of the commission protested, he backed down, still insisting that he was right. Because "America cut its eyeteeth" on discrimination against blacks, he said, if one understood that sordid history, one would also understand and know how to deal with racism against all the other groups.

Regardless of what one thinks about exceptionalism, critics of the black-white binary do make at least one valid point. The differential racialization thesis, mentioned earlier in this book (see chapter 1) and embraced by most contemporary students of race, maintains that each disfavored group in this country has been racialized in its own individual way and according to the needs of the majority group at particular times in its history. Few blacks will be yelled at and accused of being foreigners or of destroying the automobile industry. Few will be told that if they don't like it here, they should go back where they came from. Few (except those who are foreign-born) will be ridiculed on account of their unpronounceable last names or singsong accent. Few will have a vigilante, police officer, teacher, or social worker demand to see their papers, passport, or green card. Few will be asked if they are terrorists. By the same token, few Asian-looking people will be accused of being welfare leeches or having too many children out of wedlock.

Thus, different racial groups can react disparately to racial slurs [*citing cases of blacks and Mexicans subjected to racist epithets*]. . . . Due to this distinction, we hold that in an intentional infliction of emotional distress claim arising out of an allegation of racial harassment, the plaintiff's race must shape the objective inquiry into the severity of the distress.

Taylor v. Metzger, 706 A.2d 685, 698 (N.J. 1998)

Long preoccupied with issues of identity, American society prefers to place its citizens into boxes on the basis of physical attributes and culture. No science supports this practice; it is simply a matter of habit and convenience. Like other paradigms, the black-white one allows people to simplify and make sense of a complex reality. And, of course, it is helpful in looking at the historical and ongoing relationship between black and white Americans. The risk is that nonblack minority groups, not fitting into the dominant society's idea of race in America, become marginalized, invisible, foreign, un-American.

The black-white—or any other—binary paradigm of race not only simplifies analysis dangerously, presenting racial progress as a linear progression; it can end up injuring the very group, for example, blacks, that one places at the center of discussion. It weakens solidarity, reduces opportunities for coalition, deprives a group of the benefits of the others' experiences, makes it excessively dependent on the approval of the white establishment, and sets it up for ultimate disappointment. Consider some of the ways this can happen.

The history of minorities in the United States shows that while one group is gaining ground, another is often losing it. For example, in 1846 the United States waged a bloodthirsty war against Mexico in which it seized about one-half of that nation's territory. Later, Anglo lawyers and land-hungry settlers colluded with courts and local authorities to deprive the Mexicans who chose to remain in the conquered territory of their lands, which were guaranteed by the peace treaty. Yet, only a few years later, the North gallantly fought an equally bloody war against the South, ostensibly to free the slaves. During Reconstruction, slavery was abolished and important legislation enacted for the benefit of the newly freed blacks. Yet at the very same time, Congress was passing the despised Indian Appropriation Act, providing that no Indian nation would be an independent entity capable of entering into a treaty with the United States. To make matters worse, not long afterward, the Dawes Act broke up land the tribes held in common, resulting in the loss of almost two-thirds of all Indian land. And in 1882 Congress passed the Chinese Exclusion Act; earlier California had made it a crime to employ Chinese workers.

Binary thinking, which focuses on just two groups, usually whites and one other, can thus conceal the checkerboard of racial progress and retrenchment and hide the way dominant society often casts minority groups against one another to the detriment of each. Immediately after the Civil War, the army recruited newly freed slaves to serve as Buffalo Soldiers putting down Indian rebellions in the West. Not long after, southern plantation owners urged replacing their former slaves with Chinese labor. Congress acquiesced. Consider, as well, Justice Harlan's dissent in *Plessy v. Ferguson*, reproduced in part in chapter 2 of this book, which sharply rebuked segregation for blacks but supported his point by disparaging the Chinese, who did have the right to ride in railway cars with whites. In more recent times, during California's Proposition 187 campaign, proponents for this anti-immigrant measure sought black votes by depicting Mexican immigrants as newcomers who took black jobs. And in recent years, anti-immigration forces whip up public sentiment against Muslims in minority and blue-collar communities by appealing to their patriotism.

In addition to pitting one minority group against another, binary thinking can induce a minority group to identify with whites in exaggerated fashion at the expense of other groups. For example, early in California's history, Asians sought to be declared white so that they could attend schools for whites and not have to go to ones with blacks. And in the Southwest, early litigators for Mexican Americans pursued an "other white" policy, arguing that segregation of Mexican Americans was illegal because local law only countenanced segregation against blacks. Community-betterment organizations like the League of United Latin American Citizens reacted to rampant discrimination against their members by insisting that society treat Latinos as whites.

Anglocentric standards of beauty divide Mexican and black communities, enabling those who most closely conform to the Euro-American ideal to gain jobs, desirable mates, and social acceptance and, sometimes, to look down on their darker-skinned brothers and sisters. Similarly, "box checking" allows people of white or near-white appearance to gain the benefits of affirmative action without suffering the costs of being thought of and treated as black or brown.

Black-white or any other kind of binary thinking can also cause a minority group to go along with a recurring ploy in which whites select a particular group—usually a small, nonthreatening one—to serve as tokens and overseers of the others. Minorities who fall into this trap hope to gain status, while whites can tell themselves that they are not racists because they have employed a certain number of suitably grateful minorities as supervisors, assistant deans, and directors of human relations.

Finally, dichotomous thinking and exceptionalism impair the ability of groups to form coalitions. For example, neither the NAACP nor any other predominantly African American organization filed an amicus brief challenging Japanese internment in the World War II case of *Korematsu v. United States*. As mentioned earlier, a politically moderate litigation organization of Latinos distanced itself from other minority groups and even from darker-skinned Latinos by pursuing an "other white" strategy during the middle years of the twentieth century. And in Northern California, Asians, Mexican Americans, and blacks have been at loggerheads over admission to prestigious Lowell

High School and the University of California at Berkeley and UCLA.

Will minority groups learn to put aside narrow nationalisms and binary thinking and work together to confront the forces that suppress them all? It would seem that they have much to gain, but old patterns of thought die hard. If contextualism and critical theory teach anything, it is that we rarely challenge our own preconceptions, privileges, and the standpoint from which we reason.

Although not as permanent as race or color, an accent is not easily changed for a person who was born and lived in a foreign country for a good length of time. This court cannot give legal cognizance to adverse employment decisions made simply because a person speaks with a foreign accent. The court would recognize that in some instances a foreign accent may actually prevent a person from performing tasks required for employment or promotion, . . . but otherwise, an employer should not make adverse employment decisions simply because a person possesses an accent resulting from birth and life in a foreign country.

It is the court's opinion from the evidence and the observation of the plaintiff's speech at trial that his accent did not impair his ability to communicate or prevent him from performing any tasks required of the supervisor of the old dental laboratory. . . . Consequently, this court finds that the decision to demote the plaintiff from the supervisory position in the old laboratory was made on the basis of his national origin and related accent, and that this decision violated the rights of the plaintiff under the provisions of Title VII.

Carino v. University of Oklahoma, 25 Fair Empl. Proc. Cas. (BNA) 1332 (W.D. Okla. 1981)

B. Critical White Studies

Another area of critical investigation is the study of the white race. For several centuries, at least, social scientists have been studying communities of color, discoursing learnedly about their histories, cultures, problems, and future prospects. Now a new generation of scholars has put whiteness under the lens and examined the construction of the white race. If, as most contemporary thinkers believe, race is not objective or biologically significant but constructed by social sentiment and power struggle, how did the white race in America come to exist, that is, how did it come to define itself? Ian Haney López, Cheryl Harris, Tim Wise, David Roediger, Alexander Saxton, and Theodore Allen address various aspects of this issue. The physical differences between light-skinned blacks and dark-skinned whites, just to take one example, are much less marked than those that separate polar members of either group. Why then do we draw the lines the way we do? Addressing this question includes examining what it means to be white, how whiteness became established legally, how certain groups moved in and out of the white race, "passing," the one-drop rule, the phenomenon of white power and white supremacy, and the array of privileges that come with membership in the dominant race.

In the semantics of popular culture, whiteness is often associated with innocence and goodness. Brides wear white on their wedding day to signify purity. "Snow White" is a universal fairy tale of virtue receiving its just reward. In talk of near-death experiences, many patients report a blinding white light, perhaps a projection of a hoped-for union with a positive and benign spiritual force.

In contrast, darkness and blackness often carry connotations of evil and menace. One need only read *Heart of Darkness* by Joseph Conrad to see how strongly imagery of darkness conveys evil and terror. We speak of a black gloom. Persons deemed unacceptable to a group are said to be blackballed or blacklisted. Villains are often depicted as swarthy or wearing black clothing.

Whiteness is also normative; it sets the standard in dozens of situations. It may even be a kind of property interest. Other groups, such as American Indians, Latinos, Asian Americans, and African Americans, are described as nonwhite. That is, they are defined in relation or opposition to whiteness—that which they are not. Literature and the media reinforce this view of minorities as the exotic other. Minorities appear in villain roles or as romantic, oversexed lovers. Science-fiction movies and television programs portray extraterrestrials with minority-like features and skin color.

If literature and popular culture reinforce white superiority, law and courts have done so as well. In the fifty years or so following the Civil War, a large influx of people sought admission to the United States, making immigration policy a point of great concern. The last decade of the nineteenth century and first two of the twentieth were a period of particularly heavy immigration. Who was the young country going to let in? In 1790 Congress had limited naturalization (acquisition of U.S. citizenship) to free white persons only. With minor modifications, this racial qualification stood on the books until 1952.

During the more than 150 years that the requirement remained in place, U.S. courts decided many cases determining who was white and who was not. Are Indians from India white? What about Persians? Or light-skinned Japanese? Or children of mixed marriages, with a father from Canada and a mother from Indonesia? Judges developed two tests—"science" and "common knowledge"—to decide these questions. Reading the history of these strained, often overtly racist judicial opinions does much to dispel any notion that the American judiciary is fair, consistent, or wise.

The legal definition of whiteness took shape in the context of immigration law, as courts decided who was to have the privilege of living in the United States. As many ordinary citizens did, judges defined the white race in opposition to blackness or some other form of otherness, an opposition that also marked a boundary between privilege and its opposite. Only those who were deemed white were worthy of entry into our community.

> The appellant is a person of the Japanese race born in Japan [who] applied to the United States District Court for the Territory of Hawaii to be admitted as a citizen of the United States. His petition was opposed by the United States District Attorney. . . . Including the period of his residence in Hawaii appellant had continuously resided in the United States for 20 years. He was a graduate of the Berkeley, Cal., high school, had been nearly three years a student in the University of

California, had educated his children in American schools, his family had attended American churches and he had maintained the use of the English language in his home. That he is well qualified by character and education for citizenship is conceded.

The District Court . . . however, held that, having been born in Japan and being of the Japanese race, he was not eligible to naturalization under section 2169 of the Revised Statutes . . . and denied the petition. . . .

On behalf of the appellant it is urged that we should give to [section 2169] the meaning which it had in the minds of its original framers in 1790 and that it was employed by them for the sole purpose of excluding the black or African race and the Indians then inhabiting this country. . . . It is not enough to say that the framers did not have in mind the brown or yellow races of Asia. It is necessary to go farther and be able to say that had these particular races been suggested the language of the act would have been so varied as to include them within its privileges.

The appellant, in the case now under consideration . . . is clearly of a race which is not Caucasian.

Takao Ozawa v. United States, 260 U.S. 178, 189–90, 195, 198 (1922)

Another aspect of the construction of whiteness is the way certain groups have moved into or out of that race. For example, early in our history Irish, Jews, and Italians were considered nonwhite—that is, on a par with African Americans. Over time, they earned the prerogatives and social standing of whites by a process that included joining labor unions, swearing fealty to the Democratic Party, and acquiring wealth, sometimes by illegal or underground means. Whiteness, it turns out, is not only valuable; it is shifting and malleable.

A recent manifestation of white consciousness is its exaggerated form seen in white-supremacy and white-power groups. With these organizations, white solidarity presents problems and dangers that black solidarity does not. When members of a minority group band together for social and political support, most observers will see that action as a natural and proper response against social pressures. But what if members of the majority race band together to promote their interests at the expense of those very same minorities? The formation of Aryan-supremacist and skinhead groups stands as a constant reminder of how easy it is for quiet satisfaction in being white to deteriorate into extremism. As we write, the Tea Party movement and its followers are urging each other to "take back our country." Some of their rallies have featured signs lampooning President Barack Obama or depicting him with exaggerated racial features. A "birther" faction still challenges his right to hold office and insists that he prove he was born in the United States. They also urge abolishing welfare, affirmative action, and other special programs of interest to poor people and minorities of color. How much of this opposition stems from discomfort with a nonwhite leader?

"White privilege" refers to the myriad of social advantages, benefits, and courtesies that come with being a member of the dominant race. Imagine a black man and a white man, equally qualified, interviewing for the same position in a business. The interviewer is white. The white candidate may feel more at ease with the interviewer because of the social connections he enjoys as a member of the same group. The interviewer may ask the white candidate to play golf later. Under the impression that few blacks golf, and not wishing to offend, he may not invite the black candidate to play. This example becomes especially telling when one considers that most corporate positions of power, despite token inroads, are still in the hands of whites.

According to a famous list compiled by Peggy McIntosh, white people enjoy and can rely on forty-six privileges that attach by reason of having white skin, including the assurance that store clerks will not follow them around, that people will not cross the street to avoid them at night, that their achievements will not be regarded as exceptional or "credits to their race," and that their occasional mistakes will not be attributed to biological inferiority. Scholars of white privilege write that white people benefit from a system of favors, exchanges, and courtesies from which outsiders of color are frequently excluded, including hiring one's neighbors' kids for summer jobs, a teacher's agreement to give a favored student an extra-credit assignment that will enable him or her to raise a grade of B+ to A–, or the kind of quiet networking that lands a borderline candidate a coveted position.

This has prompted one commentator to remark that our system of race is like a two-headed hydra. One head consists of outright racism—the oppression of some people on grounds of who they are. The other consists of white privilege—a system by which whites help and buoy each other up. If one lops off a single head, say, outright racism, but leaves the other intact, our system of white over black/ brown will remain virtually unchanged. The predicament of social reform, as one writer pointed out, is that "everything must change at once." Otherwise, change is swallowed up by the remaining elements, so that we remain roughly as we were before. Culture replicates itself forever and ineluctably.

A version of white privilege sometimes appears in discussions of affirmative action. Many whites feel that these programs victimize them, that more qualified white candidates will be required to sacrifice their positions to less qualified minorities. So, is affirmative action a case of "reverse discrimination" against whites? Part of the argument that it is rests on an implicit assumption of innocence on the part of the white person displaced by affirmative action. The narrative behind this assumption characterizes whites as innocent, a powerful metaphor, and blacks as—what? Presumably, the opposite of innocent, namely, guilty. They are like thieves who enter where they do not belong and take things that others have worked hard for.

By contrast, many critical race theorists and social scientists hold that racism is pervasive, systemic, and deeply ingrained. If we take this perspective, then no white member of society seems quite so innocent. The interplay of meanings that one attaches to race; the stereotypes one holds of other people; the standards of looks, appearance, and beauty; and the need to guard one's own position all powerfully determine one's perspective. Indeed, one aspect of whiteness, according to some scholars, is its ability to seem perspectiveless or transparent. Whites do not see themselves as having a race but as being, simply, people. They do not believe that they think and reason from a white viewpoint but from a universally valid one—"the truth"—what everyone knows. By the same token, many whites will strenuously deny that they have benefited from white privilege, even in situations like the ones mentioned throughout this book (golf, summer jobs, extra-credit assignments, merchants who smile). (See Marianne Bertrand & Sendhil Mullainathan, Are Emily and Greg More Employable than Lakisha and Jamal?, 94 Am. Econ. Rev. 991 [Sept. 2004].)

Classroom Exercise

Imagine a Russian Jewish girl, orphaned at the age of two, who immigrates to the United States at the age of fifteen without a penny or knowledge of English. She attends night school while working as a supermarket bagger during the day and plans to attend a community college and major in premed studies.

The person is white with blue eyes and blond hair. Is she privileged? Unprivileged? Privileged in some respects but not others?

Divide into small groups and argue this question. Then ask yourselves whether white privilege has any application beyond a narrow circle of elite prep-school products.

C. *Other Developments: Latino and Asian Critical Thought, Critical Race Feminism, LGBT Theory*

As the bright lines of the black-white binary blurred, critical Asian and Latino thinkers felt freer to put forward their own unique perspectives. Invigorated, perhaps, by the antiessentialist strand of critical race theory, LatCrit scholars have called attention to such issues as immigration, language rights, bilingual schooling, internal colonialism, sanctuary for Latin American refugees, and census categories for Latinos. They have begun challenging "proxy discrimination," in which a discriminator targets a Latino on the basis of a foreign accent, name, or ancestry. They reexamine documents such as the Treaty of Guadalupe Hidalgo in search of sources of protection for land, culture, and language rights. (See *Lobato v. Taylor*, 71 P.3d 938 [Colo. 2002]; *Mabo v. Queensland*, 1991 WL 1290806 [HCA 1992].) Like Asians, many Latinos vigorously oppose the English-only movement and engage in spirited discussions of passing and assimilation (see chapter 4). They deploy the sociological notion of nativism to name and explain the recent spate of measures aimed at foreigners and immigrants, including "probable cause" laws that encourage police to stop and question the foreign-looking or to punish anyone who aids, hires, or rents an apartment to an undocumented person. They point out that nativism against Latinos and Asians thrives during times of economic hardship, when the labor supply is glutted, when workers are insecure, and when politicians rail against foreigners taking American jobs. Both groups staunchly resist the black-white paradigm but try to maintain friendly relations with African Americans. They also support immigration activists, such as the student "Dreamers" and their families who are protesting draconian immigration policies and deportation. They support histories of nonblack minority groups, such as the Ellis Island Immigration Museum's new exhibit showing stories of Mexican border-crossers and their routes and travails.

Some Asian American writers focus on accent discrimination and the "model minority myth," according to which Asians are the perfect minority group—quiet and industrious, with intact families and high academic aspiration and achievement. This myth is unfair to the numerous Asian subgroups such as Hmong and Pacific Islanders who are likely to be poor and in need of assistance. It also causes resentment among other disfavored groups, such as African Americans, who find themselves blamed for not being as successful as Asians supposedly are. ("If they can make it, why can't you?").

Allied with the model minority myth is the idea that Asians are too successful—soulless, humorless drones whose home countries are at fault for the United States' periodic economic troubles. Such was the tragic fate of the Chinese American Vincent Chin, killed in 1982 by two Detroit autoworkers upset with Japan for destroying the U.S. automotive industry by producing better cars. To make matters worse, American courts have sometimes been reluctant to punish such racially motivated crimes against Asians, handing out light sentences. For murdering Chin, the two attackers received sentences of three years' probation and small fines. Neither served a day in jail.

During World War II, when over one hundred thousand Japanese families living on the West Coast were removed to internment camps where they spent years behind barbed wire, many losing farms and businesses in the process, few Americans protested. It turned out later that much of the evidence of disloyalty and espionage was fabricated. Indeed, most Japanese Americans supported the war effort, and many young Japanese Americans served honorably in the U.S. armed forces, fighting against the Nazis in Europe and serving as interpreters in the battle against Japan. Despite this sorry chapter in U.S. history, the United States was slow to consider compensating the Japanese for their losses. The descendants of Japanese Americans endured a legacy of suspicion and prejudice. A reparations bill did not enter into force until 1988.

Gordon Hirabayashi is an American citizen who was born in Seattle, Washington, in 1918, and is currently Professor Emeritus of Sociology at the University of Alberta. He is of Japanese ancestry. In 1942 he was living in Seattle and was therefore subject to wartime orders requiring all persons of Japanese ancestry, whether citizens or not, to remain within their residences between 8:00 p.m. and 6:00 a.m. He was also subject to subsequent orders to report to a Civilian Control Station for . . . exclusion from the military area. Hirabayashi refused to honor the curfew or to report to the control station because he believed that the military orders were based upon racial prejudice and violated the protection the Constitution affords to all citizens. The Supreme Court reviewed his conviction for violating the curfew order and unanimously affirmed. . . .

In his *coram nobis* petition, Hirabayashi contended that the original report [by West Coast authorities] . . . and recently discovered related documents [proved] that the curfew and exclusion orders were in fact based upon racial prejudice rather than military exigency. . . .

The judgment . . . is reversed and the matter is remanded with instructions to grant Hirabayashi's petition to vacate both convictions.

Hirabayashi v. United States, 828 F.2d 591, 592–93, 608 (9th Cir. 1987)

Indeed, in the 2016 presidential campaign, one candidate supported his proposal to ban Muslims from admission to the United States by citing, approvingly, President Franklin Roosevelt's executive order assigning the Japanese to wartime internment camps.

Finally, in recent years a number of scholars of color have been examining issues at the intersection of feminism, sexual orientation, and critical race theory. Critical race feminism addresses issues of intersectionality, like those described in chapter 4. It also examines relations between men and women of color; sterilization of black, Latina, and Indian women; and the impact of changes in welfare, family policies, and child-support laws. It also analyzes the way the "reasonable man" standard that operates in many areas of the law incorporates a white male bias, making it difficult for a woman or a nonwhite person to receive justice in American courts.

LGBT ("queer-crit") theorists examine the interplay between sexual norms and race. Why are Latino males sometimes depicted as ardent lovers, or Asian men as sexless or effeminate? Are sex and sexual orientation part of the construction of minority racial status? And what about the civil rights movement or Chicano liberation—are they historically homophobic? Accidentally or inherently so? Are gays and lesbians marginalized by the need of these groups to appear exemplary, all-American?

QUESTIONS AND COMMENTS FOR CHAPTER V

1. If an African American asserts that, because of slavery, blacks truly are exceptional and should receive priority over other groups in jobs and social programs, is he or she asserting a form of property interest in blackness? (See Cheryl Harris, Whiteness as Property, 106 Harv. L. Rev. 1707 [1993].) Is he or she demonstrating ignorance of other groups' histories?

2. Does white privilege exist? If so, give an example. Is there such a thing as black, Chicano, or Asian privilege? How about the privilege to be uninhibitedly exuberant with one's friends?

3. If slavery is the central, foundational element in blacks' history in the United States, what serves that function for Latinos? For Indians? For Asians?

4. If it is legitimate for a school to have a black or Latino student organization, is it equally legitimate to allow white students to form a white student organization? And to use student fees to fund it?

5. Would it not be logical for blacks, Latinos, Asians, and Native Americans to unite in one powerful coalition to confront the power system that is oppressing them all? If so, what prevents them from doing so?

6. Are Latinos and American Indians exceptional? Asian Americans? Are all the groups exceptional?

7. Which groups should have a category in the U.S. Census? During certain periods, Latinos have had a category of their own, but at other times, they have not. Are they a race? An ethnicity? What is a Hispanic?

8. Should multiracial people have a census category? Several? How many?

9. Suppose that a Latino worker's coworkers make fun of his lunch food, calling him a "taco eater." They also joke about his family's being "wetbacks" and his friends "lettuce pickers." (See *Alvarado v. Shipley Donut Flour & Supply Co., Inc.*, 526 F. Supp. 2d 746 [S.D. Tex. 2007]; *Lopez v. Union Car. Co.*, 8 F. Supp. 2d 832 [N.D. Ind. 1998]; *Machado v. Goodman Mfg. Co.*, 10 F. Supp. 2d 709 [S.D. Tex. 1997].) Is this racial discrimination for which the worker can sue under a federal civil rights statute? If your answer is no, is that because you have adopted, whether you realize it or not, a black-white binary paradigm of race?

10. Is a police program that keeps an eye on Muslims and mosques racist? Or is it merely a sensible measure aimed at improving the security of all Americans? Will it go down in history as a shameful action like Japanese internment?

SUGGESTED READINGS

Allen, Theodore, The Invention of the White Race, Vols. 1–2 (1994, 1997).

Brooks, Roy L. & Kirsten Widner, In Defense of the Black/White Binary: Reclaiming a Tradition of Civil Rights Scholarship, 12 Berkeley J. Afr.-Am. L. & Pol'y 107 (2010).

Critical White Studies: Looking behind the Mirror (Richard Delgado & Jean Stefancic eds., 1997).

Delgado, Richard, Derrick Bell's Toolkit: Fit to Dismantle That Famous House?, 75 N.Y.U. L. Rev. 283 (2000).

Feagin, Joe R., The White Racial Frame: Centuries of Racial Framing and Counter-framing (2009).

Gomez, Laura, Manifest Destinies: The Making of the Mexican American Race (2007).

Haney López, Ian F., White by Law: The Legal Construction of Race (10th Anniversary ed., 2006).

Harris, Cheryl I., Whiteness as Property, 106 Harv. L. Rev. 1707 (1993).

Ignatiev, Noel, How the Irish Became White (1995).

Isenberg, Nancy, White Trash: The 400-Year Untold History of Class in America (2016).

McIntosh, Peggy, White Privilege and Male Privilege: A Personal Account of Coming to See Correspondences through Work in Women's Studies (1988).

Perea, Juan F., The Black/White Binary Paradigm of Race, 85 Cal. L. Rev. 1213 (1997).

Roediger, David R., The Wages of Whiteness: Race and the Making of the American Working Class (paperback ed., 2007).

Ross, Thomas, Innocence and Affirmative Action, 43 Vand. L. Rev. 297 (1990).

Saucedo, Leticia, The Browning of the American Workplace, 80 Notre Dame L. Rev. 303 (2004).

Takaki, Ronald T., Strangers from a Different Shore: A History of Asian Americans (rev. ed., 1998).

Valdes, Francisco, Queers, Sissies, Dykes, and Tomboys: Deconstructing the Conflation of "Sex," "Gender," and "Sexual Orientation" in Euro-American Law and Society, 83 Calif. L. Rev. 1 (1995).

Wildman, Stephanie, with contributions by Margalynne Armstrong, Adrienne D. Davis & Trina Grillo, Privilege Revealed: How Invisible Preference Undermines America (1996).

Williams, Robert A., Linking Arms Together: American Indian Visions of Law and Peace (rev. ed. 1999).

Wise, Tim, Dear White America: Letter to a New Minority (paperback ed., 2012).

Wu, Frank, Yellow: Race in America beyond Black and White (paperback ed., 2003).

CHAPTER VI

Critiques and Responses to Criticism

As Thomas Kuhn has shown, paradigms resist change. It should come as no surprise, then, that critical race theory, which seeks to change the reigning paradigm of civil rights thought, has sparked stubborn resistance. During the movement's early years, the media treated critical race theory relatively gently. As it matured, however, critics felt freer to speak out. Some of the areas that drew critical attention are storytelling; the critique of merit, truth, and objectivity; and the matter of voice. Many of these early critiques are cited in the list of readings at the end of this chapter. Here we take up only a few.

A. "External" Criticism

Among the initial critiques, one by Randall Kennedy and another by Daniel Farber and Suzanna Sherry are notable. Kennedy took issue with the idea that minority scholars speak in a unique "voice" about racial issues. He also took the movement to task for accusing mainstream scholars of ignoring the contributions of writers of color, an accusation that found its most forceful expression in Richard Delgado's "Imperial Scholar" article. Kennedy reasoned that legal scholarship is like a marketplace. Good articles and books attract "buyers"—recognition, citation, reprintings. Thus, pointing out that certain texts have fallen into a void does not, by itself, prove discrimination. It is first necessary to establish that those articles were of high quality and deserved recognition. Kennedy thus charged the crits with failing to examine their premises and painting themselves as victims when they had not shown that they deserved better treatment than they had received.

For their part, Farber and Sherry accused critical race theorists of hiding behind personal stories and narratives to advance their points of view, as well as lacking respect for traditional notions of truth and merit. Citing the example of Jews and Asians—two minority groups that have achieved high levels of success by conventional standards—they argued against the idea that the game is rigged against minorities. If conventional tests and standards are unfair and biased against minorities, as the crits assert, how can one account for the success of these two groups? Did they cheat or take unfair advantage? Are they unimaginative mimics and drones? All possible explanations are implausible. Therefore, CRT's critique of merit is implicitly anti-Semitic and anti-Asian.

The crits' responses were not long in coming. In a series of articles, including a special colloquy in the *Harvard Law Review*, critical race theorists and their defenders argued that Randall Kennedy himself was guilty of misstatement and an unsympathetic reading of CRT texts. Because Kennedy approached the new movement through conventional criteria, he missed opportunities to help take racial analysis to a new level.

As for Farber and Sherry, the crits replied that if Asians and Jews succeeded despite an unfair system, this is all to their credit. But why should pointing out unfairness in universal merit standards, like the Scholastic Aptitude Test (SAT), bespeak a negative attitude toward members of those groups? As the crits saw it, Farber and Sherry confused criticism of a standard with criticism of individuals who performed well under that standard. Judge Richard Posner and the *New Republic* writer Jeffrey Rosen also took issue with the crits along predictable lines.

Recently, the right wing has mounted a furious attack on civil rights and critical race theory, with conservative bloggers, talk-radio hosts, and devotees of color blindness leading the way. With the advent of the Obama presidency, detractors have stepped up their assault, some trying to link the nation's first black president with the critical race theory guru Derrick Bell, who taught at Harvard during the time when the young Obama studied law there. Many of them charged that with his presidency, the nation had overcome its racist past and that no further efforts were necessary. Any more would amount to catering to undeserving minorities. Whether the United States is now a postracial society is now a prime point of contention.

B. *"Internal" Criticism*

In addition to responding to outside criticism, critical race theory has engaged in intensive self-criticism, often outside the public view. This critique takes two forms, one having to do with the pragmatic, on-the-ground value of critical race theorizing, the other with the worth of the theories themselves.

1. The Activist Critiques

Is critical race theory pragmatic? Some of the issues that arise in the internal critique (self-criticism) are ones any new movement might expect to address. What is its practical worth? Why is it not down in the trenches, helping activists deal with problems of domestic violence, poor schools, and police brutality? Why is it so hard on liberals or so disdainful of existing civil rights statutes and remedies? What is the purpose of critique unless one has something better to replace it with? Should crits work together in an interracial coalition or separately, with blacks and Latinos, for example, pursuing slightly different agendas? Should whites be welcome in the movement and at its workshops and conferences? Should the critical race theory movement expand to include religious discrimination, against Jews and Muslims, for example? To the extent that a cohesive set of answers has emerged from self-criticism, one may summarize by noting that most crits agree that theory and practice need to work together. Street activists, for their part, need new theories to challenge a social order that treats minority communities and the poor so badly. By the same token, theorists need the infusion of energy that comes from exposure to real-world problems, both as a galvanizing force for scholarship and as a reality test for their writing.

As for criticizing the existing system, the crits respond that they are indeed at work developing a vision to replace it. As examples, they cite Derrick Bell's theories of cultural and educational self-help; Lani Guinier's efforts to reform electoral democracy; Charles Lawrence's, Mari Matsuda's, and Richard Delgado's work developing a new theory of hate speech; Juan Perea's arguments for linguistic pluralism; and Devon Carbado's and Mitu Gulati's analyses of workplace discrimination.

A jury found that defendants had engaged in employment discrimination, in part by permitting plaintiffs to be the target of racial epithets repeatedly spoken by a fellow employee. In addition to awarding damages, the trial court issued an injunction prohibiting the offending employee from using such epithets in the future. Defendants argue that such an injunction constitutes a prior restraint that violates their constitutional right to freedom of speech. For the reasons that follow, we hold that a remedial injunction prohibiting the continued use of racial epithets in the workplace does not violate the right to freedom of speech if there has been a judicial determination that the use of such epithets will contribute to the continuation of a hostile or abusive work environment and therefore will constitute employment discrimination.

Aguilar v. Avis Rent a Car System, Inc., 21 Cal. 4th 121, 126; 980 P.2d 846, 848 (1999)

2. Critique of the Intellectual Heart of the Movement

Other questions go to the intellectual heart of critical race theory. A persistent internal critique accuses the movement of straying from its materialist roots and dwelling overly on matters of concern to middle-class minorities—microaggressions, racial insults, unconscious discrimination, and affirmative action in higher education. If racial oppression has material and cultural roots, attacking only its ideational or linguistic expression is apt to do little for the underlying structures of inequality, much less the plight of the deeply poor.

Another concern that some crits raise is that the movement has become excessively preoccupied with issues of identity, as opposed to hard-nosed social analysis. Armchair issues such as the social construction of race, the role of multiracial people, "passing," and endless refinements of the antiessentialist thesis may pose intriguing intellectual puzzles, but they lie far from the central issues of our age. It seems difficult to imagine W. E. B. Du Bois, if he were alive today, writing a Ph.D. dissertation on passing or on whether a professor should be able to earn tenure on the basis of an article written entirely in the narrative voice. By the same token, it may be that lavish attention to the nuances of intersectional identity and the differences in perspective that separate, say, mixed-race women of Samoan-white parentage and black-looking, Spanish-speaking men from Brazil is less worthy than it was in early years. A furious right-wing attack on all people of color and the poor has, perhaps, rendered these differences less relevant than they were in former times. In general, the internal critiques go only to the movement's emphasis and allocation of resources and attention. They do not threaten its solidarity, vitality, or ability to generate vital insights into America's racial predicament (see chapter 7).

A further internal critique raises the question of whether critical race theory takes adequate account of economic democracy. If the emerging issues of the new century are world trade, globalization, workers' rights, and who shares in the new wealth created by the technology revolution, a movement that has no theory of race and class is apt to seem increasingly irrelevant. The recent series of economic shocks heightens the need for such an inquiry. If racism is largely economic in nature—a search for profits—and hypercapitalism is increasingly showing itself as a flawed system, what follows for a theory of civil rights?

C. Critical Race Theory as a Method of Inquiry in New Fields and Countries

A final set of critiques question whether critical race theory or particular tools in its arsenal are still helpful or likely to remain so when they are exported to areas outside the setting (namely, domestic, U.S. racism in its late-1980s manifestations). Justin Driver, for example, has questioned whether Derrick Bell's interest-convergence formula (see chapter 2) has any continuing validity. And a host of scholars in other disciplines or countries, while enthusiastically embracing the new perspectives CRT offers, advocate caution in extending it to new settings, such as the caste system in India or the Roma ("gypsies") in Europe.

By the same token, American crits and their supporters may do well to follow carefully the alterations and advances that their counterparts in Europe, Canada, Australia, and Latin America are making. For example, British scholars in the field of education are developing intriguing analyses of class and maintaining lively exchanges with Marxist scholars, something that has been missing in the American scene, at least to date.

Classroom Exercise

The program coordinator for the regional conference on critical race theory seeks your advice on the following question: The conference committee wishes to include a two-hour session, toward the end of the conference, dealing with extremely sensitive internal criticism of the direction the movement has been taking. Should the session be open or closed to the press? Should it be open only to persons who have participated in the movement for at least five years? Should whites be excluded? Should the organizers ask the participants to refrain from recording it?

In other words, what should one do about airing "dirty laundry"? One half of your group argues the let-it-all-hang-out position, while the other argues for a secret session. (See John Calmore, Airing Dirty Laundry: Disputes among Privileged Blacks—From Clarence Thomas to the Law School Five, 46 How. L.J. 175 [2003].)

QUESTIONS AND COMMENTS FOR CHAPTER VI

1. Reconsider the question posed at the end of chapter 1: Is critical race theory too pessimistic?

2. Do CRT's critics make the mistake of holding up the new paradigm of civil rights thought to the standard of the old one? Is this like deeming Martin Luther a heretic because he sought to change the teachings of the Catholic Church or like judging Jesus by the standards of the Roman Empire?

3. Is it problematic that before a certain point, most of the civil rights literature in law was written by a small circle of white scholars who cited mainly each other and ignored the small, but growing, literature written by scholars of color? Or might it have one or more perfectly logical explanations?

4. Are stories based on firsthand experience—for example, racial discrimination at a department store—irrefutable (because only the author was there), and, if so, how can other scholars build on or criticize them? Are they power moves? Exclusionary? Useful raw experience or data?

5. Is it a waste of time for a movement that seeks social justice to focus on internal issues of identity and the relations of subgroups within itself?

6. Is working within the system or outside it the best way to bring about change? Which would you choose, and why?

7. If Group A (say, Jews) is successful and Group B (say, blacks) is not, and Group B charges that the system is rigged, is that an implied criticism of Group A, because it implies that they took advantage of an unfair system to get ahead?

SUGGESTED READINGS

Colloquy, Responses to Racial Critiques of Legal Academia, 103 Harv. L. Rev. 1844 (1990).

Delgado, Richard, The Imperial Scholar: Reflections on a Review of Civil Rights Literature, 132 U. Pa. L. Rev. 561 (1984).

Driver, Justin, Rethinking the Interest Convergence Thesis, 105 Nw. U. L. Rev. 149 (2015).

Farber, Daniel & Suzanna Sherry, Beyond All Reason: The Radical Assault on Truth in American Law (1997).

Johnson, Alex M., Jr., The New Voice of Color, 100 Yale L.J. 2007 (1991).

Kennedy, Randall L., Racial Critiques of Legal Academia, 102 Harv. L. Rev. 1745 (1989).

Posner, Richard A., The Skin Trade, New Republic, October 13, 1997, at 40.

Rosen, Jeffrey, The Bloods and the Crits, New Republic, December 9, 1996, at 27.

Tushnet, Mark, The Degradation of Constitutional Discourse, 81 Geo. L.J. 151 (1991).

Critical Race Theory Today

What is the situation of critical race theory today? In some respects, the movement is thriving. Dynamic sub-disciplines, such as the Latino-critical movement, queer-crit (LGBT) studies, and a fledgling group of Muslims with a critical orientation challenge civil rights thinkers to reconsider the ways they conceptualize equality, civil rights, and national security. Critical race theory is taught at many law schools and has spread to other disciplines and countries. Some judges incorporate its ideas into opinions, often without labeling them as such. Lawyers use critical race theory techniques to advocate on behalf of clients and to expose bias within the system. In this chapter, we discuss some of these developments and the impact that CRT seems to be having on national discourse. We analyze some of the internal struggles that are playing out within the group and examine a few topics, such as class, poverty, the wealth and income gaps, crime, campus climate, affirmative action, immigration, and voting rights, that are very much on the country's front burner.

A. Right-Wing Offensive

The decade of the nineties saw the beginning of a vigorous offensive from the political Right. Abetted by heavy funding from conservative foundations and position papers from right-wing think tanks, conservatives advanced a series of policy initiatives, including campaigns against bilingual education, affirmative action, employment and educational set-asides, and immigration. They also lobbied energetically against hate-speech regulation, welfare, and governmental measures designed to increase minorities' political representation in Congress. Some of the backers of these conservative initiatives were former liberals disenchanted with the country's departure from color-blind neutrality. Others were nativists concerned about immigration or national security hawks worried about the threat of terrorism.

Critical race theorists took part in all those controversies. They also addressed identity issues within critical race theory, intergroup coalitions, and the use of empirical methods in theorizing and confronting discrimination.

B. Front-Burner Issues

Though the American economy advanced rapidly during the Reagan and Clinton years, it began sagging with the dot-com bust and later the bursting of the housing bubble and collapse of the finance industry during the Bush years. Without training in the emerging fields of technology and global marketing, minority communities had begun falling further and further behind. But with the economic downturn and weak recovery that followed, they fell even further. They had few natural allies. The Democratic Party courted them less assiduously than it had in former times; the labor movement had lost force; and the country lacked the spur of Cold War competition to enforce antidiscrimination norms rigorously. Postracialism and neoliberal politics that sought to split the difference ("triangulate") between conservative and liberal policies did little to relieve black misery. Politicians and TV ideologues inveighed against the evils of undocumented immigration, heightening suspicion of Latinos, even ones whose families had been here for generations. After 9/11, Muslims fared even worse, including a rain of insults, surveillance, and even physical attacks on Middle Eastern–looking persons and mosques.

In such an atmosphere, many critical thinkers put their minds to the task of combating what they saw as the country's long slide into racial indifference, even hostility.

1. Race, Class, Welfare, and Poverty

A field on which ideological battles rage is the distribution of material benefits in society. This controversy shades off into the much-debated question of whether race or class is the dominant factor in the subjugation of people of color. Is racism a means by which whites secure material advantages, as Derrick Bell proposed? Or is a "culture of poverty," including broken families, crime, intermittent employment, and a high educational dropout rate, what causes minorities to lag behind?

Critical race theory has yet to develop a comprehensive theory of class. A few scholars address issues such as housing segregation in terms of both race and class, show-ing that black poverty is different from almost any other kind. Real estate steering, redlining, and denial of loans and mortgages, especially after the end of World War II, prevented blacks from owning homes, particularly in desir-able neighborhoods. These practices also excluded blacks from sharing in the appreciation in real estate property values that some eras have witnessed. Confinement to cer-tain neighborhoods, in turn, limits where black and Latino parents may send their children to school and so perpetu-ates the cycle of exclusion from opportunities for upward mobility that have enabled many poor whites to rise.

Some race crits focus on discrimination in higher-echelon jobs and in such fields as the delivery of health services. The critique of standardized testing also contains a class element: critics of tests such as the SAT have shown that many of the questions are class bound, requiring familiarity with such items as polo mallets or regattas, and that the best predictor of a person's SAT score is his or her father's occupation; another is his or her zip code.

Other critical race theorists ponder the distribution of environmental dangers and biohazards. The environ-mental justice movement analyzes a type of internal colo-nialism, in which installations such as toxic-waste sites, radioactive tailings, and sewage-treatment plants are dis-proportionately placed in or near minority communities or on Indian reservations. Inadequate or poisoned water systems seem almost always to sicken the occupants of cities like Flint, Michigan, not Beverly Hills or Scarsdale. Corporate defenders of these practices argue, as they do in the international arena, that they are merely going to the best market. Sometimes they point out that minority communities welcome the jobs that a sewage-treatment plant, for example, would bring. Civil rights activists reply that the marketplace is far from neutral and that a corporation that takes advantage of a community's financial vulnerability is engaging in predatory behavior, if not outright racism. They note that global warming is producing flooding in impoverished native villages in Alaska and small islands in the far Pacific. A dynamic example of critical race theory in action, the environmental justice movement aims at forging a coalition between the hitherto white-dominated conservation movement and minority communities. If it succeeds, it will have created a truly powerful force for change.

I concur in Chief Judge Wilkinson's well-reasoned opinion of the court. I write separately, however, to memorialize my serious concern with the shabby treatment the African-American residents of Jersey Heights have suffered at the hands of state and federal highway planners and officials.

It is no historical accident that Jersey Heights today is ninety-nine percent African-American. Displaced from their downtown neighborhoods by the construction of Route 13 in the 1930s and the original Route 50 in the 1950s, African Americans in Salisbury relocated to Jersey Heights. As a result of widespread steering practices, Jersey Heights was the only area in which Salisbury's African Americans could find available housing. According to one plaintiff, Salisbury has had an "unwritten law"—that "if you were a certain pigmentation you had to live west of this [Wicomico River] bridge." . . .

> Although the term "environmental justice" is of fairly recent vintage, the concept is not. See Michele L. Knorr, Environmental Injustice, 6 U. Balt. J. Envtl. L. 71, 73–76 (1997).
>
> As Ms. Knorr aptly states, "environmental health hazards are unequally distributed in the United States. Millions of people in minority and low-income communities are subjected to greater levels of pollution than Caucasian and wealthy populations because of their race or socioeconomic status. Environmental injustice occurs, in part, because of the exclusion of these communities in the decision-making process as well as the disproportionate location of pollution." Knorr, Environmental Injustice, U. Balt. J. Envtl. L. at 71–72 (footnotes omitted).
>
> As Justice Douglas pointed out nearly thirty years ago, "as often happens with interstate highways, the route selected was through the poor area of town, not through the area where the politically powerful people live."
>
> *Jersey Heights Neighborhood Ass'n v. Glendening, 174 F.3d 180, 186 n.1 (4th Cir. 1999)*

How should critical observers see the increasing disparity between the household incomes and assets of the top 10 percent of our society and all the rest? Formerly, the United States relied on redistributive measures such as a progressive income tax, public education, and a welfare safety net to prevent people at the bottom from slipping into permanent poverty. Today, those programs command much less support than they did formerly. Some writers believe that the reason is that the public sees the recipients of welfare as having black and brown faces—even though more whites receive welfare than do people of color. In short, society tolerates poverty and blighted prospects for outsider groups.

Many critical race scholars recognize that poverty and race intersect in complex ways, so that the predicament of very poor minority families differs in degree from that of their white counterparts. White poverty—except, perhaps, for the rural kind—usually lasts only for a generation or two, even for white immigrant families. Not so for black or brown poverty—it is apt to last forever. By the same token, middle-class or professional status for blacks, browns, or American Indians is less secure than for others. Their children can fall from grace with breathtaking speed; sometimes all it takes is one arrest or a few very low grades in school. But a general theory of race and economics remains elusive, at least for now. Interest in the topic is rising, however, especially among the millennial generation of young adults.

In the meantime, a few legal scholars have been pointing out how universal programs such as the G.I. Bill, federal housing supports, or even Social Security end up widening the gap between whites and blacks. The programs fall on already-plowed ground. Whites are more able to take advantage of them than blacks are. Sometimes the programs contain hidden preferences and assumptions that enable whites to benefit more from them than people of color can. The same is likely to happen if society retires affirmative action based on race for a version based on socioeconomic disadvantage, as many writers have suggested. This approach is popular with defenders of the color-blind approach—scholars and commentators who wish that society would stop thinking in terms of race but instead focus on efficiency, class, merit, and other means of ordering society.

2. Policing and Criminal Justice

Another set of contemporary issues has to do with addressing racism in the criminal justice system. On any given day, over 60 percent of the black men in the District of Columbia are enmeshed in that system—in jail or prison, on probation or parole, or wanted on a warrant. In East Los Angeles, 50 percent of young Mexican American men suffer the same fate. Black men who murder whites are executed at a rate nearly ten times that of whites who murder blacks. And as most readers of this book will know, the number of young black men in prison or jail is larger than the number attending college.

Many progressive people seek to understand the meaning of these figures and search for ways to combat the conditions that create them. Critical race theory's contribution has taken a number of forms. Building on the work of radical criminologists, one race crit shows that the disproportionate criminalization of African Americans is a product, in large part, of the way we define crime. Many lethal acts, such as marketing defective automobiles, alcohol, or pharmaceuticals or waging undeclared wars, are not considered crimes at all. By the same token, many things that young black and Latino men are prone to do, such as congregating on street corners, cruising in low-rider cars, or scrawling graffiti in public places, are energetically policed, sometimes under new ordinances that penalize belonging to a gang or associating with a known gang member. Crack-cocaine offenses still receive harsher penalties than those for powder cocaine. Figures show that white-collar crime, including embezzlement, consumer fraud, bribery, insider trading, and price fixing, causes more deaths and property loss, even on a per capita basis, than does all street crime combined.

Other CRT scholars address racial profiling, in which the police stop minority-looking motorists to search for drugs or other contraband, and "statistical discrimination" carried out by ordinary people who avoid blacks or Latinos because they believe they are more likely than whites to be perpetrators of crime or members of vicious gangs. Both practices penalize law-abiding people of color and alienate the young.

The 48 declarations submitted by the City in support of its plea for injunctive relief paint a graphic portrait of life . . . in an urban war zone. The four-square-block neighborhood, claimed as the turf of a gang variously known as Varrio Sureño Town, Varrio Sureño Treces (VST), or Varrio Sureño Locos (VSL) is an occupied territory. Gang members . . . congregate on lawns, on sidewalks, and in front of apartment complexes at all hours of the day and night. They display a casual contempt for notions of law, order, and decency— openly drinking, smoking dope, sniffing toluene, and even snorting cocaine laid out in neat lines on the hoods of residents' cars. The people who live in Rocksprings are subjected to loud talk, loud music, vulgarity, profanity, brutality, fist-fights and the sound of gunfire echoing in the streets. . . . Area residents have had their garages used as urinals; their homes commandeered as escape routes; their walls, fences, garage doors, sidewalks, and even their vehicles turned into a sullen canvas of gang graffiti.

. . . The people of this community are prisoners in their own homes.

People ex rel. Joan R. Gallo v. Acuna, 14 Cal. 4th 1090, 929 P.2d 596, 601 (1997) (upholding an injunction against members of an alleged "criminal street gang" under which the youths—all or most of whom were Latinos—would be forbidden from gathering with each other or their friends in a public place)

Other critical race scholars urge jury nullification to combat the disproportionate incarceration of young black men. In this practice, the jury, which in most large cities will contain people of color, uses its judgment, sometimes ignoring instructions from the judge, on whether to convict a defendant who has committed a nonviolent offense, such as shoplifting or possession of a small amount of drugs. If the jury believes that the police system is racist or that the young man is of more use to the community free than behind bars, it will vote to acquit. (See also discussion of antisnitching campaigns in chapter 4.)

One federal judge, versed in critical race theory, applied a similar analysis in the case of a black defendant. Under a three-strikes-and-you're-out type of law, the judge was required to sentence the man to a long term. On noticing that the man's two previous offenses had been automobile connected, the judge declined to do so. Reasoning that racial profiling by the police causes black motorists to be pulled over more frequently than whites, she concluded that the defendant's two prior convictions had likely been tainted by racism. Consequently, she sentenced him to the shorter term appropriate for nonrepeat offenders.

> The scholarly and popular literature strongly suggest . . . racial disparity in the rates at which African Americans are stopped and prosecuted for traffic offenses. That literature, together with the specific facts about Leviner's record and background, compel me to depart from the Guidelines range. . . .
>
> While the Sentencing Guidelines were designed to eliminate unwarranted disparities in sentencing, and constrain a judge's discretion, they are not to be applied mechanistically, wholly ignoring fairness, logic, and the underlying statutory scheme. . . .
>
> Motor vehicle offenses, in particular, raise deep concerns about racial disparity. Studies from a number of scholars, and articles in the popular literature have focused on the fact that African American motorists are stopped and prosecuted for traffic stops, more than any other citizens. And if that is so, then it is not unreasonable to believe that African Americans would also be imprisoned at a higher rate for these offenses as well.
>
> *Judge Nancy Gertner in United States of America v. Leviner, 31 F. Supp. 2d 23, 24, 25, 33 (D. Mass. 1998)*

Still others examine the recent wave of prison building, including the outsourcing of incarceration to private entrepreneurs. They analyze who profits from this social trend. They also question why sentences in the United States are so long—among the longest in the world—and punitive in orientation rather than rehabilitative. The Prison-to-College Pipeline, initiated by the John Jay College of Criminal Justice, seeks to help inmates acquire skills that will enable them to make a successful reentry to postprison life.

States are beginning to heed these suggestions, in part out of interest convergence. In many states, the prisons are so crammed full that judges have ordered early release for some prisoners. A few states pay so much to operate their prison system—an amount nearly equal to what they spend on public education—that their budgets are under severe strain.

One scholar, Paul Butler, proposes that the values of hip-hop music and culture could serve as a basis for reconstructing the criminal justice system so that it is more humane and responsive to the concerns of the black community. That program of reconstruction needs to start soon. Police shootings and killings of unarmed black men have risen so rapidly that even a leading medical journal recognizes them as growing health concerns. Civil rights scholars, crits, and community activists have been demanding changes in police training and culture, and civilian review boards. A vigorous "Black Lives Matter" movement has been pressing for change. Many campus activists have taken up the cause, as well.

Imprisonment for a felony often leads to disenfranchisement under state laws that deprive felons of the right to vote, even after serving their time. We take up the question of voting rights in a subsequent section.

3. Hate Speech, Language Rights, and School Curricula

Additional issues have to do with speech and language. One of the first critical race theory proposals had to do with hate speech—the rain of insults, epithets, and name-calling that many minority people face on a daily basis. An early article documented some of the harms that this type of speech can inflict. It pointed out that courts were already affording intermittent relief for victims of hate speech under such doctrines as defamation, intentional infliction of emotional distress, and assault and battery and concluded by urging a new independent tort in which the victims of deliberate, face-to-face vituperation could sue and prove damages.

Later articles and books built on this idea. One writer suggested criminalization as an answer; others urged that colleges and universities adopt student conduct rules designed to deter hate speech on campus. Still others connected hate speech to the social-construction-of-race hypothesis, pointing out that concerted racial vilification contributes to social images and ingrained preconceptions of people of color as indolent, immoral, or intellectually deficient. Although occasional plaintiffs have gained relief through the tort avenue, U.S. courts have treated campus hate-speech codes harshly, striking down at least four as violations of the First Amendment. Elsewhere, however, the Supreme Court of Canada upheld that country's criminal-hate-speech provision, citing U.S. critical race theorists' work, while many European and British Commonwealth countries have instituted controls similar to Canada's.

On the premise that "legal realism" will soon reach First Amendment jurisprudence, sweeping aside mechanical rules and barriers ("no recovery for mere offense") in favor of a broader, more policy-sensitive approach, critical race theorists have been tackling some of the most common policy objections to hate-speech regulation, including that more speech is the best remedy for bad speech, that hate speech serves as a pressure valve relieving tension that might explode in an even more harmful manner later, and that a focus on speech fails to get at the "real problem." In the meantime, American courts, seemingly influenced by critical race theory writing, have been upholding causes of action brought by minority victims of hate speech under such legal theories as hostile environment.

In 1972, plaintiff Carrie Taylor began working as a sheriff's officer in the office of the Burlington County Sheriff. On January 31, 1992, Taylor, who is African American, was at the Burlington County Police Academy for firearms training.

. . . While there, she encountered defendant Henry Metzger and Undersheriff Gerald Isham. Taylor said hello, and, in response, Metzger turned to Isham and stated: "There's the jungle bunny." Isham laughed. Plaintiff believed the remark to be a demeaning and derogatory racial slur, but she did not reply. She became a "nervous wreck," immediately began crying, and went to the bathroom.

In this case, defendant's remark had an unambiguously demeaning racial message that a rational factfinder could conclude was sufficiently severe to contribute materially to the creation of a hostile work environment. The term . . . "jungle bunny" is patently a racist slur, and is ugly, stark and raw in its opprobrious connotation. . . . See Mari Matsuda, Public Response to Racist Speech, 87 Mich. L. Rev. 2330, 2338 (1989) ("However irrational racist speech may be, it hits right at the emotional place where we feel the most pain.").

Taylor v. Metzger, 706 A.2d 685, 691 (N.J. 1998)

As this book went to press, students on several dozen campuses were demonstrating for "safe spaces" and protection from racially hostile climates with daily insults, epithets, slurs, and displays of Confederate symbols and flags. Some campuses are reevaluating the possibility of rules and policies aimed at protecting equal educational opportunity. These "campus climate" issues are prompting serious reconsideration among university administrators, and for good reason. With affirmative action under sharp attack, universities need to assure that their campuses are as welcoming as possible. At the same time, a new generation of millennials seems to be demonstrating a renewed willingness to confront illegitimate authority.

Hate speech on the Internet is posing a difficult problem. Blogs, tweets, cartoons (for example, of a disliked figure, such as the Prophet Muhammad), and other messages in this medium are inexpensive and easy to circulate, often anonymously. They enable those who dislike a person or race to find others of like mind, so that reinforcement builds, often unopposed. Society polarizes, with groups distrusting each other and believing the other side wrongheaded. Of course, counterspeech is easy and inexpensive on the Internet. Still, the ready availability of an avenue for replying to a vituperative message has not completely solved the problem.

A second speech-related issue concerns the rights of non-English speakers to use their native languages in the workplace, voting booth, schoolhouse, and government offices. This issue, of great concern to Asian and Latino populations, squarely confronts a growing tide of nativist sentiment that also includes immigration controls and restrictions on the provision of government services to noncitizens. Crits point out that language is an essential part of culture and identity, that having a French or British accent is deemed a mark of refinement, not a sign of deficiency, and that many foreign countries are happily multilingual and not at all balkanized. Although over half of American states have enacted English-only measures over the past two decades, the tide may be turning: the Arizona State Supreme Court recently declared unconstitutional that state's harshly enforced official-English statute as a violation of the First Amendment.

> At the outset, we note that this case concerns the tension between the constitutional status of language rights and the state's power to restrict such rights. On the one hand, in our diverse society, the importance of establishing common bonds and a common language between citizens is clear. . . . We recognize that the acquisition of English language skills is important in our society. . . .
>
> However, the American tradition of tolerance "recognizes a critical difference between encouraging the use of English and repressing the use of other languages." . . . If the wide-ranging language of the prohibitions contained in the Amendment

> were to be implemented as written, the First Amendment
> rights of [non-English speakers] would be violated.
>
> *Arizona Supreme Court, in striking down that state's English-*
> *only amendment, in Ruiz v. Hull, 957 P.2d 984, 990, 991 (Ariz.*
> *1998)*

In 2006, Arizona voters passed a new English-only law designed to meet the court's objections.

Arizona, of course, has been the site of considerable anti-immigrant ferment. With a large Spanish-speaking population and a long border with Mexico, the state recently enacted one of the country's most overtly anti-immigrant laws. A 2010 statute empowered local police to request documentation of immigration status from persons with whom they come into contact and suspect may be undocumented. The state boasted, as well, a large and shifting contingent of unofficial border vigilantes who claimed to assist law enforcement in reporting and arresting unofficial entrants. Many carried out their functions with a zeal that suggested that their main motivation is dislike of the foreign-born, even law-abiding individuals merely looking for honest work. The state overplayed its hand: the bill was so heavy-handed that the Supreme Court struck down most of it. Not deterred, the Arizona legislature enacted a second bill eliminating courses of Mexican American Studies (MAS) in schools like those in Tucson. The Tucson program had been popular and so successful that over 90 percent of its students graduated, many going on to college. The anti-MAS statute is also under review right now (see chapter 4).

4. Affirmative Action and Color Blindness

When Martin Luther King, Jr., issued his famous call for America to put aside its racist past and judge people not by the color of their skin but by the content of their character, he was echoing a demand with long roots in America's history. More than half a century earlier, in *Plessy v. Ferguson*, Justice John Harlan in a famous dissent protested the majority's formalistic separate-but-equal decision. In *Plessy*, a black man had challenged a railroad's rule prohibiting him from riding in a car reserved for whites. The railroad replied that it had set aside identical cars for black passengers, and, hence, its practice did not violate the Equal Protection Clause of the Fourteenth Amendment. The Supreme Court agreed with the railroad, establishing the principle of separate-but-equal that lasted until the *Brown* decision of 1954.

Justice Harlan's scathing dissent rebuked the majority's decision. He pointed out that history and custom rendered preposterous the blithe denial that anything impermissible had happened. The railroad's separation of the races occurred against a background that made its symbolism and insult unmistakable. With *Brown v. Board of Education*, the judicial system moved away from its earlier interpretation of equality, adopting Justice Harlan's position. The new approach, which looked not merely to whether a law or practice mentioned race but to its real-world effects, lasted through the sixties and seventies. During this time, the nation adopted affirmative action, which arrived with President Lyndon Johnson's Executive Order 11246 in 1965. Soon a host of federal and state agencies, including schools and universities, followed suit.

By the midseventies, affirmative action had become so unpopular in certain circles that Alan Bakke, who had been denied admission to the University of California at Davis Medical School, sued to declare race-conscious admissions in higher education unconstitutional. The Supreme Court's splintered decision narrowed affirmative action by insisting that universities set aside no formal quota for minorities and that they compare every candidate with every other. If universities were careful to observe these limitations, they could consider race as one factor among many in order to achieve a diverse intellectual environment. Although subsequent decisions cast doubt on this so-called diversity rationale, a Supreme Court decision from Michigan, *Grutter v. Bollinger*, reaffirmed *Bakke*'s essential lesson. Public universities, if they see fit, may operate narrow affirmative action programs aimed at creating a diverse intellectual climate.

Conservatives, however, have not abandoned the struggle. Beginning with position papers, op-ed columns, and books, writers of this persuasion have been arguing that affirmative action balkanizes the country, stigmatizes minorities, violates the merit principle, and constitutes reverse discrimination. Some, such as the authors of *The Bell Curve*, have even argued that minorities may be biologically inferior to whites, so that disparate representation in selective schools and occupations should come as no surprise. Conservatives followed up their media campaign with a series of public referenda and initiatives aimed at declaring affirmative action illegal in particular states.

Civil rights organizations and progressive educators have sought to counter each of these efforts. Progressive scientists challenged the premises of *The Bell Curve* and similar neoeugenicist tracts, showing how they rest on discredited science. Critical race theorists have launched a thoroughgoing attack on the idea of conventional merit and standardized testing. Conservatives make points by charging that affirmative action gives jobs or places in academic programs to individuals who do not deserve them. The public receives incompetent service, while better-qualified workers or students are shunted aside. This argument has resonated with certain liberals who equate fairness with color blindness and equal opportunity, rather than equal results (see chapter 2).

CRT's critique of merit takes a number of forms, all designed to show that the notion is far from the neutral standard that its supporters imagine it to be. Several writers critique standardized testing, demonstrating that tests like the SAT or LSAT are coachable and reward people from high socioeconomic levels who can afford to pay for expensive test-prep courses (see chapter 6). Law-test scores predict little more than first-year grades—and those only modestly—and do not measure other important qualities such as empathy, achievement orientation, or communication skills. These writers point out that merit is highly situational. If one moves the hoop in a basketball court up or down six inches, one radically changes the distribution of who has merit. Similarly, if one defines the objective of a law school as turning out glib lawyers who excel at a certain type of verbal reasoning, then one group would appear to have a virtual corner on merit. But if one defines lawyering skills more broadly to include negotiation, inter-personal understanding, and the ability to craft an original argument for law reform, then a different group might well emerge.

A UCLA educator, Richard Sander, advanced a different critique. He argues that affirmative action in law schools merely places blacks in settings where they are in over their heads and fail at high rates. Without the lift of the unseen hand, minorities would attend schools further down the pecking order and be happier and more successful. Defenders counter that minority graduates of top schools who were admitted under affirmative action programs are, on the whole, well adjusted and successful in school and in later life. These schools have more resources, alumni networks, and smaller classes than ones further down the line, so that students of color who enroll there generally have good experiences and go on to contribute significantly to society.

Some current critics urge abolishing race-based affirmative action in favor of a version based on economic class. Such a program, they say, would help all kids who grew up poor, not just minorities. It would also be in harmony with the current vogue of color-blind remedies and approaches to race and racism. Most educators, however, believe that such a shift would devastate the chances of communities of color, because the number of poor whites greatly exceeds that of poor minorities. One scholar proposed that any institution tempted to implement an affirmative action plan of this type also take into account advantage, or white privilege (see chapter 5). For example, imagine a university admissions committee comparing two candidates. Candidate A is a Chicano from East Los Angeles with a 3.9 grade point average from an inner-city school and an SAT score of 1050. His college essay recounts that he stepped in when his father went to jail and helped raise his younger siblings. His life objective is to apply César Chávez's religion-based, collectivist ideas to organize urban neighborhoods.

Candidate B is a son of a white, suburban family who sent him to a private school and to Europe during his junior year. This student has a 3.3 grade point average from an elite school and an SAT score of 1200. He has no particular educational objective but wants to develop an all-around grounding in liberal arts before going to work in his dad's company. His personal essay describes how his effort to make the junior-varsity cross-country team strengthened his character.

Most admissions officers, like most readers of this book, would undoubtedly favor the Chicano candidate despite his lower test scores, but why? Perhaps it is because we believe that Candidate B has not made the most of his opportunities, while Candidate A seems eager to do so. The author who developed this proposal drew on notions of white privilege to urge that admissions officers discount, or penalize, the scores of candidates like B, thus clearing a way for ones like A. This measure would reduce the number of lackadaisical admits, clearing the way for even larger numbers of students of all races who have suffered real disadvantage and are eager to further their education.

Recently, mainstream organizations, including the American Bar Association, have been considering deemphasizing standardized tests, including the SAT and its law-school version, the LSAT, on the grounds that they only imperfectly predict occupational or professional success and discriminate against minorities.

In order to cultivate a set of leaders with legitimacy in the eyes of the citizenry, it is necessary that the path to leadership be visibly open to talented and qualified individuals of every race and ethnicity. All members of our heterogeneous society must have confidence in the openness and integrity of the educational institutions that provide this training. . . . Access to legal education (and thus the legal professions) must be inclusive of talented and qualified individuals of every race and ethnicity, so that all members of our heterogeneous society may participate in the educational institutions that provide the training and education necessary to succeed in America.

Grutter v. Bollinger, 539 U.S. 306, 332–33 (2003)

5. Globalization and Immigration

A fifth issue that is very much at the forefront of critical race theory currently is international globalization. A globalizing economy removes manufacturing jobs from inner cities (often to other countries), creates technology and information industry jobs for which many minorities have little training, and concentrates capital in the pockets of an elite class, which seems little inclined to share it. A globalizing economy often includes free-trade agreements, like NAFTA, which can decimate the economies of a weaker nation such as Mexico. At the same time, however, globalization offers opportunities for minorities to form coalitions with American blue-collar workers and unions that face similar issues—loss of jobs and a weakening wage structure. Some crits believe that the situations of domestic minorities and peer workers in Third World countries are linked and must be addressed together and that hypercapitalism is doomed to produce periodic crises and financial downturns during which minority fortunes, like those of the working poor, suffer. The development of *maquiladoras* on the Mexican side of the U.S. border brings many of these problems into high relief.

History suggests that the scholars who call attention to these global developments may be right. Sweatshop and other exploitive conditions in overseas factories generally afflict poor, formerly colonized people of color, many of them women. Decontextualized free-market ideology would hold that American corporations are merely offering these workers the going wage or maybe even slightly better. Critics point out that the reason these wages are low and the new jobs attractive is that U.S. and European colonialism has robbed the former colonies of their natural wealth, suppressed the development of local leaders, and conspired with right-wing dictators to keep the people poor, fearful, and disorganized. Indian leaders such as Rigoberta Menchú and Subcomandante Marcos have led resistance movements in many Latin American countries, calling attention to the need for economic democracy and land reform. American corporations often oppose these changes. Many Latino-critical scholars and even Pope Francis have taken stands in support of the indigenous movements.

If the materialist wing of critical race theory is right, domestic minorities have suffered at the hands of very similar forces. Indeed, their fates are linked with those of their overseas counterparts, since capitalists can always use the threat that industrial operations will relocate overseas to defeat unions, workplace regulations, welfare, and other programs of interest to U.S. minorities. Accordingly, some crits have begun reading or rereading the body of literature known as postcolonial studies in an effort to understand how their movement might dovetail with these other forces.

Another prominent area for critical race analysis is immigration law. The United States tolerates and, in some cases, abets repressive murderous regimes abroad, often in small countries whose wealth it and other colonial powers have already plundered. People from these countries, unsurprisingly, often want to immigrate to the United States or to the prosperous industrialized countries of northern Europe. Although the United States dropped its racist national-origin quota system in 1965, it still limits immigration and polices the southern border with Mexico zealously. Judicial review of immigration policy is sharply limited because of the plenary power doctrine, under which courts grant Congress virtually unlimited power to regulate immigration. Thus, treatment of countries or groups of would-be immigrants that would constitute clear-cut equal protection or due process problems cannot be challenged in court. The resulting harsh treatment of people fleeing poverty, gangs, death squads, or repression in their home countries offers what one critical race theorist has called a "magic mirror" into the heart of America. This mirror shows how American society really thinks of its own citizens of color and would treat them if it were not for the courts.

As we write, civil rights scholars have been challenging racial profiling of Latino-looking immigrants, local ordinances aimed at immigrants, lawless border vigilantes, and the privatization of immigration detention. They also have been asking who benefits from increased immigration enforcement and prison building. They have also been questioning whether the high degree of suspicion and surveillance that the national intelligence establishment devotes to Middle Eastern–looking people and Muslims is merited or even makes sense in law enforcement terms. It alienates the very community whose cooperation the authorities need in keeping tabs on threats to national security. It allows real terrorist groups in the Middle East to make propaganda capital at our expense. And it recalls unsavory chapters in U.S. history such as World War II–era internment of an entire domestic minority merely on the basis of the suspicion that a small subgroup might be harboring unpatriotic thoughts and plans. One recent scholar notes the way presidential rhetoric in the War on Terror echoes old themes from the days of Indian frontier wars.

6. Voting Rights

As mentioned, aggressive policing and incarceration create large numbers of civilians who are ex-cons and unable to vote. But in addition to "felon disenfranchisement," communities of color suffer another kind simply by reason of their numerical minority status. In most elections, except for those of mayors of certain large cities, people of color will be in the minority. Even if they vote as a bloc, if whites vote that way as well, minorities are apt to be outvoted.

The Supreme Court has recently approved voting requirements that have a disproportionate effect on minority voting. Until the country's demographic makeup shifts even more decisively, efforts must continue to counter minority underrepresentation. Cumulative voting, proposed by a leading critical race theorist, would circumvent some of these problems by allowing voters facing a slate of ten candidates, for example, to place all ten of their votes on one, so that if one of the candidates is, say, an African American whose record and positions are attractive to that community, that candidate should be able to win election. The same author has provided a number of suggestions aimed at ameliorating the predicament of the lone black or brown legislator who is constantly outvoted in the halls of power or is required to engage in exchanges of votes or favors to register an infrequent victory.

With recent cutbacks in the protection of minorities in voting (*Shelby County v. Holder*), all these matters take on increased urgency. Since 2013, southern officials no longer need to secure federal "preclearance" when they change voting rules. Many have seized on this opportunity to require photo identification, relocate registration offices to distant locales, and limit voting hours in ways that are likely to fall heavily on minority citizens wishing to vote.

C. Identity

As mentioned earlier (see chapter 2), a great divide separates two broad types of current critical race scholarship. One (the materialist or "real world" school) writes about issues such as globalization, immigration, nativism, the wealth divide, race and class, and the criminal justice system. In broad agreement with Derrick Bell's view of race as expressing material interests of elite groups, members of this persuasion set out either to understand, analyze, criticize, or change conditions that afflict communities of color in their effort to secure better, more prosperous lives.

Discourse analysts, by contrast, focus on ideas and categories by which our society constructs and understands race and racism. Writers in this camp are apt to emphasize issues, such as identity and intersectionality, that center on categorical thinking. They are likely to examine the role of ideas, thoughts, feelings, unconscious discrimination, stereotype threat, and implicit associations and their implications for judicial reasoning. The lines are not rigid; some writers ponder, for example, both hate speech and the social construction of race, or unconscious discrimination and the overt, in-your-face kind. For example, the second group of scholars has conducted a lively round of discussions dealing with relations inside critical race theory itself, questioning, for example, whether the "essential" LatCrit is a deeply religious Catholic. If so, how does that affect gay or lesbian Latinos/as whose lifestyle has been firmly marginalized by that church? Others analyze the internal makeup of the Latino group, many of whom have an indigenous heritage as well as a European one. Should they designate themselves as "Indian" on U.S. Census forms? Should they check the "other race" box and, in the space following it, write in the word "mestizo"? We have already mentioned the controversy over whether American racial thought incorporates a black-white binary. If so, does attachment to that binary marginalize Asians, Latinos, and American Indians? Is it, in short, a power move? Do all people of color share something in common, namely, their oppression, or can we only speak of oppressions?

Meanwhile, some crits in the materialist group are growing impatient with the discourse analysts, urging that the country's racial predicament is becoming so acute that devoting energy to how a few highly placed university professors relate to each other or the terms in which they speak is like Nero's fiddling while Rome burns. The discourse analysts, for their part, point out that many of our chains are mental and that we will never be free until we throw off ancient restrictions and demeaning patterns of thought and speech and create the discourse to talk about necessary new concepts.

Despite occasional disagreements and differences of emphasis, critical race theory remains a dynamic force on the

American legal and cultural scene. The formation of spin-off groups, far from impairing the group's effectiveness or muting its voice, has only added new, vital dimensions to the movement as a whole.

Classroom Exercise: Panel on the Intersection of Race and Body Image

This time you are the program coordinator for the regional student conference on critical race theory. You have just received a letter from a group at one of the area's schools that wishes to have a panel on eating disorders and body image. They point out that eating disorders and body-image distortions are a major source of unhappiness among people of color, both young and old, and that the pressure to conform to Eurocentric standards of beauty and physical appearance makes these problems especially acute for minority women, many of whom have little chance of meeting them (see chapter 5). You are concerned that the press, which is sure to cover your conference, will have a field day with the fatness panel if you allow it to go on.

The class or study group is your program committee. Elicit the pros and cons of the proposal and decide how to deal with it.

D. Critical Empirical Analysis

In recent years, psychologists and other social scientists have been developing new tools to understand racial oppression and its effects. On the basis of work by Claude Steele, Joshua Aronson, and others, empiricists have

attempted to learn how stereotype threat impairs the a\
ity of minority test-takers to do their best work and how
to combat it. To this point, courts have been slow to apply
the teachings of this new form of knowledge, even though
it would seem to promise insight into the reasons for the
minority-white test gap.

> Due to the sparseness of the evidence . . . the court is unable
> to determine whether stereotype threat explains any part of
> the gap between Caucasian and underrepresented minority
> LSAT scores. . . . Professor Steele does not quantify the effect
> of stereotype threat; nor, at least according to this report, has
> he performed any research on the LSAT. If there is evidence
> showing that stereotype threat accounts for some of the LSAT
> gap, it was not produced in this case.
>
> The . . . argument . . . assumes all members of the under-
> represented minority groups have suffered adversity entitling
> them to some degree of upward adjustment in their UGPA
> and LSAT scores. . . . Every law school applicant is an individ-
> ual whose personal history is unique. . . . [T]he court is unable
> to determine whether stereotype threat explains any part of
> the gap between Caucasian and underrepresented minority
> LSAT scores.
>
> *Grutter v. Bollinger, 137 F. Supp. 821 (E.D. Mich. 2002)*

Other social psychologists study implicit associations,
the near-automatic connections that almost every person
who grows up in American society draws between race
and personal qualities, such as cleanliness, attractiveness,
goodness, and a tendency to obey the law. Many Americans have taken the implicit association test, which is
online, and learned that they harbor negative attitudes

toward minorities, foreigners, or women. Unlike stereo-type threat, implicit association research has been slowly making inroads into the thinking of lawyers and judges.

> Testimony that educates a jury on the concepts of implicit bias and stereotypes is relevant to the issue of whether an employer intentionally discriminated against an employee. . . .
>
> Rule 702 simply requires that: (1) the expert be qualified; (2) the testimony address a subject matter on which the factfinder can be assisted by an expert; (3) the testimony be reliable; and (4) the testimony "fit" the facts of the case. . . .
>
> All of these factors are satisfied here. Dr. Greenwald is qualified. His opinions are based on reliable methodologies and consist of relevant subject matter. Finally, Dr. Greenwald's testimony is likely to provide the jury with information that it will be able to use to draw its own conclusions. Therefore, the Court finds that, provided sufficient foundation is laid at trial, Dr. Greenwald's expert testimony is helpful enough to survive the admissibility threshold.
>
> *Samaha v. Wash. St. Dept. of Tran., U.S. Dist. Ct., E.D., Wash.,*
> *Jan. 3, 2012, WL 11091843 at 4.*

Still others have been applying social-dominance theory and the work of Jim Sidanius and his colleagues in an effort to understand why humans seem to exhibit a drive to control and dominate their fellow citizens. And a few build on the work of Charles Pierce and Peggy Davis to theorize how microaggressions construct a world in which minorities and women are constantly on the defensive. A handful of court opinions dealing with workplace discrimination find that a constant rain of small insults on the job amounts to redressable discrimination.

QUESTIONS AND COMMENTS FOR CHAPTER VII

1. Now that you have come this far, revisit the question with which chapter 2 began: Would a determined campaign by every white person in this country to be color blind—to completely ignore the race of other people— eliminate the scourge of racism and racial subordination? Or is racism so embedded in our social structures, rules, laws, language, and ways of doing things that the system of white-over-black/brown/yellow subordination would continue, as though on autopilot? Is racial subordination so profitable and familiar that society is unlikely ever to give it up?

2. A majority of people of color support affirmative action; a majority of whites oppose it. Why is that?

3. Does affirmative action reward incompetence? If so, why has the country's productivity not slipped during the twenty-five years that the program has been in operation? And why do most large corporations favor it?

4. Why should a light-skinned son of a black neurosurgeon with an SAT score of 1080 get the nod over the daughter of a Ukrainian immigrant who works in a furniture factory, had to learn English from scratch, and earned a score of 1250?

5. If the police stop black male motorists 50 percent of the time and whites only 10 percent of the time and justify those stops by pointing out that black males commit more crime than whites, is that fair?

6. If a white police officer sees two young black or Latino males walking down the sidewalk with no obvious destination or reason for being there, is it OK for the officer to ask them where they are going? Is it insulting and disrespectful to do so, even if the officer asks politely?

7. The nation's prisons and jails are full of minority inmates, especially young men. Is that racist, and if so, what should be done about it?

8. How do you feel about black jurors who engage in jury nullification? Did our system do something similar in the South when courts failed to convict white killers of black civil rights protesters?

9. If corporations and government agencies locate 50 percent of the biohazards (such as sanitation plants) in minority communities and 10 percent in white ones, is that fair? Suppose that land is cheaper in the minority neighborhood, so that the decision seems economically rational. Is that a good reason for locating these facilities there? Suppose that minority people have flocked to these areas because of the well-paying jobs they offer or because housing is cheaper there.

10. If a U.S. corporation pays a Thai woman $1.10 per hour to work a ten-hour shift in a hot, noisy factory, and the prevailing rate in Thailand is $1.00 per hour for an eleven-hour workday, is that fair? Suppose that she insists that she wants to work there? What is a fair minimum wage in a developed country such as the United States?

11. Blacks, Chicanos, and Asians are constantly outvoted by whites in elections, but is anything wrong with that? Shouldn't the majority rule?

12. Latinos are now 17 percent of the U.S. population and outnumber blacks as the largest ethnic minority group. Where do Latinos figure into the civil rights equation? Are they more like blacks? Whites? American Indians? Asian Americans? And who decides? Should they qualify for affirmative action and other government programs?

13. Many of us like to think that society is less racist now than before, at least in a raw sense. But hate speech seems to be increasing in the age of blogs, websites, and talk radio. If so, what is the solution? Don't conservative radio personalities and anonymous users of the Internet have the right to say what they think?

14. The British and French colonial administrators wielded power over large native populations through a variety of strategies, including co-opting local elites by giving them midlevel jobs in the colonial administration and preaching Western superiority. Now that the U.S. population is beginning to resemble that of a colonial state, with a minority of whites and a preponderance of people of color, will these same neocolonial strategies find use once again? Is this already happening?

15. Most people today believe that hate speech ought to be discouraged. Even if one is angry at another individual, we think it is wrong to call him by a name marking an ethnic slur ("You ____"). Suppose a

rapper uses the same word. Is that hate speech? Why or why not?

16. What should a social activist do if his or her school or other organization refuses to hire minorities, denies domestic-partner benefits to gay couples, and refuses to explore renewable sources of energy to run its campus or building?

SUGGESTED READINGS

Alarcón, Daniel, Laws across the Country Are Being Used to Target Young Men Who Look Like Gang Members, but What If They Aren't What They Seem?, N.Y. Times Mag., May 31, 2015, at 47.

Alexander, Michelle, The New Jim Crow: Mass Incarceration in the Age of Colorblindness (2010).

Armour, Jody D., Negrophobia and Reasonable Racism (1997).

Blow, Charles M., Confederate Flags and Institutional Racism, N.Y. Times, June 24, 2015.

Butler, Paul, Let's Get Free: A Hip-Hop Theory of Justice (2009).

Carney, Zoe Hess & Mary E. Stuckey, The World as the American Frontier: Racialized Presidential War Rhetoric, 80 S. Comm. J. 163 (2015).

Cole, Luke & Sheila Foster, From the Ground Up: Environmental Racism and the Rise of the Environmental Justice Movement (2000).

Crenshaw, Kimberlé, The First Decade: Critical Reflections, or "A Foot in the Closing Door," 49 UCLA L. Rev. 1343 (2002).

Davis, Peggy C., Law as Microaggression, 98 Yale L.J. 1559 (1989).

Delgado, Richard & Jean Stefancic, Hate Speech in Cyberspace, 49 Wake Forest L. Rev. 319 (2014).

Erman, Sam & Gregory M. Walton, Stereotype Threat and Antidiscrimination Law: Affirmative Steps to

Promote Meritocracy and Racial Equality in Education, 88 S. Cal. L. Rev. 307 (2015).

Gilreath, Shannon, The End of Straight Supremacy: Realizing Gay Liberation (2011).

Gulati, Mitu & Patrick S. Shin, Showcasing Diversity, 89 N.C. L. Rev. 1017 (2011).

Hernández, Tanya Katerí, Afro-Mexicans and the Chicano Movement: The Unknown Story, 92 Cal. L. Rev. 1537 (2004).

Johnson, Kevin R., Opening the Floodgates: Why America Needs to Rethink Its Borders and Immigration Laws (2007).

Matsuda, Mari J., Public Response to Racist Speech: Considering the Victim's Story, 87 Mich. L. Rev. 2320 (1989).

Perea, Juan F., Demography and Distrust: An Essay on American Language, Cultural Pluralism, and Official English, 77 Minn. L. Rev. 269 (1992).

Perez Huber, Lindsay & Daniel Solorzano, Racial Microaggressions as a Tool for Critical Race Research, 18 Race, Ethnicity, and Educ. 297 (2015).

Pruitt, Lisa R., Who's Afraid of White Class Migrants? On Denial, Discrediting, and Disdain (and Toward a Richer Concept of Diversity), 31 Colum. J. Gender & L. 196 (2015).

Russell-Brown, Katheryn, The Color of Crime: Racial Hoaxes, White Fear, Black Protectionism, Police Harassment, and Other Macro-Aggressions (2d ed., 2008).

Sander, Richard, A Systemic Analysis of Affirmative Action in American Law Schools, 57 Stan. L. Rev. 367 (2003).

Simon, Jonathan, Mass Incarceration on Trial (2014).

When Markets Fail: Race and Economics (Emma Coleman Jordan & Angela P. Harris eds., 2006).

Yamamoto, Eric K., Reframing Redress: A "Social Healing through Justice" Approach to United States–Native Hawaiian and Japan-Ainu Reconciliation Initiatives, 16 Asian Am. L.J. 5 (2009).

Conclusion

Chapter 7 described critical race theory today. Now, it is time to offer some thoughts on the future. This will include hazarding some predictions on the range of problems that civil rights activists and theorists may face as well as the choices for tackling them. Finally, we consider how the establishment may react to some of the movement's efforts.

A. The Future

Imagine a young, female child born in the year 2017. She might be white, black, brown, Asian, or mixed race. The color does not matter. Her religion might be Christian, Jewish, Muslim, Buddhist, or atheist. What sort of world will she inherit? During her early years, the number of blacks and Latinos will be almost equal, with Asians a fast-growing minority as well. Whites, however, will continue to be in the numerical majority until about 2042 and will remain the largest single group into the foreseeable future.

At first, our child is apt to grow up in a segregated neighborhood and attend segregated schools. Courts have been ending desegregation decrees, while conservatives have been lobbying effectively for the end of affirmative action in higher education—and may succeed despite the Supreme Court's ruling upholding that practice in Fisher v. University of Texas. U.S. wealth is sharply split between a very well-to-do group at the top of the socioeconomic ladder and everybody else. If our child is lucky enough to be born into a well-to-do family, she may grow up in a gated community with excellent services, schools, and private security forces. If not, she will live—if white—at a level roughly comparable to a midlevel European country, such as Spain or Italy, or a struggling Third World country, if black or brown. The new economy, based on information technology and a large service sector, will do little to alter this distribution of wealth and influence.

A few decades later, as our child is approaching adulthood, conditions may change. U.S. minorities of color will grow in numbers and begin, for the first time, to pose political and economic competition for whites. The number of minority judges, business executives, and politicians holding elective office will inexorably increase. At the same time, globalization and the need to cultivate business with developing countries will begin to place a premium on multicultural, multiracial people who can speak other languages and interact easily with their foreign counterparts. Minorities will find new niches in the world economy.

Will this power shift occur peacefully or only after a long struggle? The reader's guess is as good as ours. One school of social science holds that socioeconomic competition heightens racial tensions, at least in the short run.

At the same time, interest-convergence theory suggests that as the world becomes more cosmopolitan and minority status and linguistic competence evolve into positive assets, the opposite may occur, much as it has done during wartime. (See Philip A. Klinkner & Rogers M. Smith, The Unsteady March: The Rise and Decline of Racial Equality in America [1999].) If so, barriers against minority home ownership, job mobility, and entry to universities and colleges may ease somewhat. Colleges and workplaces will try new programs to increase the flow of minorities into the market; scholars and lawyers will find new legal theories, acceptable to courts, allowing this to happen. Workplaces will heed the call of Devon Carbado and Mitu Gulati and stop pressuring minority workers to perform extra work on the job concealing their blackness or brownness and reassuring their fellow workers that they are not frightening, foreign, or incompetent. With luck, our hypothetical child, toward the end of her life, will experience a peaceful transition to a more inclusive, polyglot America. A third Reconstruction, somewhat along the lines of the 1960s, may take place, but more slowly, surely, and irreversibly.

B. A Critical Race Agenda for the New Century

Of course, the peaceful transition just described may not take place—the white establishment may resist an orderly progression toward power sharing, particularly in connection with upper-level and technical jobs, police agencies, and government. As happened in South Africa, the change may be convulsive and cataclysmic. If so, critical theorists and activists will need to provide criminal defense for resistance movements and activists and to articulate theories and strategies for that resistance. Or a third, intermediate regime may set in. As mentioned earlier, whites may deploy neocolonial mechanisms, including token concessions and the creation of a host of light-skinned minority middle managers to stave off the transfer of power as long as possible.

But, assuming that the transition proceeds and is relatively peaceable, civil rights activists and scholars will need to address a host of issues as the United States changes complexion. These include the continued deconstruction of race, so that biological theories of inferiority and hierarchy cannot ever again arise. They include further efforts to erase barriers to upward mobility for minority populations, especially old-fashioned tests and standards for merit, such as the SAT, that currently stand in the way. Prompted by critical theorists, some schools are doing this now.

Those efforts will include measures, such as economic boycotts, aimed at increasing minority representation in the media as well as countering publishers, writers, cartoonists, and movie producers who continue to distribute demeaning caricatures of minorities. They include rectifying racism in policing and the criminal justice system, so that young minority men have a better chance of going to college than to jail. They will include, as well, sentencing reform and attention to postconviction consequences such as felony disenfranchisement that otherwise will haunt an offender for the rest of his or her life. The needed efforts will include assuring that minority viewpoints and interests are taken into account, as though by second nature, in every major policy decision the nation makes.

Critical race theorists will need to take part in the development of new immigration policies that allow a freer flow of workers and capital, while assuring that the new arrivals do not enter on terms that weaken the ability of current workers to unionize and seek workplace reforms. Immigration law's defects will need attention so that people, including young, often unaccompanied, children, escaping totalitarian regimes do not end up in large detention centers or deported back to whence they came, suffering nightmares, impaired cognitive development, other psychic ills, and even death in the process.

These activists will need to assure that society cease requiring assimilation as a ticket for admission to jobs, neighborhoods, and schools and that minorities who choose to retain their culture, language, accent, religion, or ways of dress may do so without penalty. They will need to pursue zealously the goal of economic democracy, so that the currently disproportionate numbers of people of color who suffer intense poverty receive a decent level of services, health care, and education so that they—or, at least, their children—have a chance of taking part in mainstream American life. They will need to clarify, as well, the relationship between race and class as separate but overlapping vectors of disadvantage.

Above all, they will need to marshal every conceivable argument, exploit every chink, crack, and glimmer of interest convergence to make these reforms palatable to a majority that only at a few times in its history has seen fit to tolerate them; then they will need to assure, through appropriate legislation and other structural measures, that the reforms cannot easily be undone. This may necessitate making connections with counterparts in foreign countries so as to draw on their experiences and learn from each other.

C. Likely Responses to the Critical Race Theory Movement

Assuming that the future goes roughly as we have outlined—with difficulty, resistance, and thinly veiled repression in the short run but broader vistas beginning a few decades in the future—and assuming that CRT takes on many of the tasks outlined in the preceding section, what does the future hold for CRT as a movement? A number of options seem possible.

1. Critical Race Theory Becomes the New Civil Rights Orthodoxy

CRT could become the new civil rights orthodoxy. The voter-representation schemes (including cumulative voting, described in chapter 7) put forward by Lani Guinier and others could be enacted, assuring a larger number of mayors, senators, and members of Congress of color. Courts could soften their approach to hate-speech regulation, as urged by authors such as Mari Matsuda, Charles Lawrence, and Richard Delgado, perhaps realizing that an increasingly multicultural society cannot tolerate concerted marginalization and revilement of a substantial segment of its membership. Nativism against Latinos might ease, and the nation may adopt a new, more liberal immigration policy. The critique of color blindness may, one day, persuade the U.S. Supreme Court to accept race-conscious measures in employment and education, leveling the playing field for those who have long been excluded from society's bounty. A new "Americanized" federal Indian law policy, as advocated by Robert Williams, might recognize Indian tribes, unequivocally, as sovereign nations. The nation might begin considering reparations toward this group, as well as toward blacks, whose ancestors were enslaved, and Chicanos and Puerto Ricans, whose lands were taken and homelands colonized.

Critical race theory may even follow the example of critical legal studies (CLS), which embedded itself so thoroughly in academic scholarship and teaching that its precepts became commonplace, part of the conventional wisdom. This may, in fact, be happening. Consider how in many disciplines scholars, teachers, and courses profess, almost incidentally, to embrace critical race theory. Consider as well how many influential commentators, journalists, and books, such as Michelle Alexander's *The New Jim Crow*, develop critical themes while hardly mentioning their origins in critical thought. Might critical race theory one day diffuse into the atmosphere, like air, so that we are hardly aware of it anymore?

2. Critical Race Theory Marginalized and Ignored

The new race scholars could also be ignored, as they were in the movement's early days (see chapter 1). Presidents, college faculties, and commissions on race could go back to seeking counsel from the voices of incrementalism and color blindness, perhaps out of a desire to engage in denial or to "keep the lid on" as long as possible.

3. Critical Race Theory Analyzed but Rejected

The movement has already drawn its share of detractors who see it as overly radical, inconsistent with Enlightenment philosophy, and a bad example to minority communities. More could be persuaded to this point of view, especially if right-wing talk radio and websites continue to proliferate and gain popularity, or if the country's party politics shift radically.

4. Partial Incorporation

A perhaps more likely outcome is that some aspects of critical race theory will be accepted by society's mainstream and halls of power, while other parts of it will continue to meet resistance. The narrative turn and storytelling scholarship seem well on their way toward acceptance, as does the critique of merit. The rise of social media has only accelerated these trends. Intersectionality seems well entrenched in women's studies and other disciplines. More radical features, such as recognition that the status quo is inherently racist, rather than merely sporadically and accidentally so, seem less likely to gain acceptance. The need for regulation of hate crime and speech will probably become evident, as it has to dozens of European and Commonwealth nations.

If even these relatively mild insights of critical race theory are adopted, however, the effort will not have been in vain. American society, not to mention its intellectual community, seems receptive to thinking (if not acting) more creatively about race. Certainly, mainstream liberal civil rights law has been generating little excitement, nor has it provided much in the way of support for minority communities in great need of it. Perhaps if outsider scholars—and new converts and fellow travelers—persist, their work in time will come to seem not so strange or even radical, and change may come to American society, however slowly and painfully.

Virginia's statute does not run afoul of the First Amendment insofar as it bans cross burning with intent to intimidate. Unlike the statute at issue in *R.A.V.*, the Virginia statute does not single out for opprobrium only that speech directed toward "one of the specified disfavored topics." It does not matter whether an individual burns a cross with intent to intimidate because of the victim's race, gender, or religion, or because of the victim's "political affiliation, union membership, or homosexuality." . . .

The First Amendment permits Virginia to outlaw cross burnings done with the intent to intimidate because burning a cross is a particularly virulent form of intimidation. . . . Virginia may choose to regulate this subset of intimidating messages in light of cross burning's long and pernicious history as a signal of impending violence.

Virginia v. Black, 538 U.S. 343, 344–45 (2003)

Classroom Exercise

Write down five predictions for how you see America's racial scene developing twenty-five years from now. Put this paper in a safe place for future reference. Before doing so, compare notes with three other persons in your class or study group. How many of your predictions overlap? Possible areas you may wish to consider: Will the United States ever have a black woman president? (In the first edition of this book, we asked how soon readers thought a black president would arrive.) A Latino/a? An Asian American? A gay, lesbian, or transgender leader?

Will the United States ever have open immigration, or will it take the opposite tack of greatly limiting immigration? Will minority numbers really exceed those of whites midway in the twenty-first century, as many demographers believe, and what will happen then? Will race and racism ever disappear? Will the Human Genome Project show that the eugenicists and race-IQ researchers were at least partly right and that real, nontrivial differences do mark the races? Intermarriage between blacks and whites is now very low—on the order of a few percent of all marriages. Will this increase? Will a crisis cause all racialized minorities to unite in a broad, powerful coalition—and, if so, what sort of crisis could produce that result? Suppose the country absorbs a second major terrorist strike. What will it do to your predictions?

1. It is said that the arrow of progress is as often backward as forward. Which of the scenarios described in this chapter—or yet some other—do you see as most likely for America's racial future?

2. What role do you see for leftist political theory, such as CRT, in the years ahead? What role do you see for yourself?

3. The philosopher Søren Kierkegaard once said that we are doomed to lead life forward but only to understand it backward, that is, in retrospect. Is this more or less true of relations among the races? (See chapter 2, discussing the "empathic fallacy.")

4. Critical race theory is expanding into other countries and academic disciplines, such as ethnic studies, political science, women's studies, and American studies. It is also beginning to change how we approach crime, policing, and sentencing policy. Will the same happen, after a time, in other societies such as China and Indonesia and other disciplines such as medicine?

5. Two crits (Devon Carbado and Mitu Gulati) point out that minority workers often find themselves performing "extra work" when they devote much time and energy to reassuring white fellow workers that they are just like them, that is, are not threats, inscrutable, or seething under the surface and have the same range of interests as they do and so on. Suppose the balance tips, so that

whites are in a minority in the workplace. Will whites have to engage in "performative identity," perhaps in order to reassure their colleagues of color that they are hip, cool, and musical, too?

SUGGESTED READINGS

Bowen, William G. & Derek Bok, The Shape of the River: Long-Term Consequences of Considering Race in College and University Admissions (1998).

Brooks, Roy L., Atonement and Forgiveness: A New Model for Black Reparations (2006).

Carbado, Devon W. & Cheryl Harris, The New Racial Preferences, 96 Cal. L. Rev. 1139 (2008).

Charting the Future of College Affirmative Action (Gary Orfield, Patricia Marin, Stella M. Flores & Liliana M. Garces eds., 2007).

Critical Race Studies program (UCLA School of Law), http://www.law.ucla.edu/home/index.asp?page=1084.

cummings, andré douglas pond, A Furious Kinship: Critical Race Theory and the Hip-Hop Nation, 48 U. Louisville L. Rev. 499 (2010).

Hochschild, Jennifer L., Looking Ahead: Racial Trends in the United States, 134 Daedalus 70 (Winter 2005).

How Race Is Lived in America (series), N.Y. Times, June 4, 5, 7, 11, 14, 16, 20, 22, 25, 29; July 2, 6, 9, 13, 2000, http://www.nytimes.com/race.

Oliver, Melvin L. & Thomas M. Shapiro, Black Wealth / White Wealth: A New Perspective on Racial Inequality (2d ed., 2006).

Our Next Race Question: The Uneasiness between Blacks and Latinos, Harper's, April 1996, at 55.

Warren, Elizabeth, The Economics of Race: When Making It to the Middle Is Not Enough, 61 Wash. & Lee L. Rev. 1771 (2004).

Wilkins, David E. & K. Tsianina Lomawaima, Uneven Ground: American Indian Sovereignty and Federal Law (2002).

Glossary of Terms

ACCENT DISCRIMINATION: Discrimination, for example, by an employer against a worker, on the basis of a foreign-sounding accent; or the assumption that native English speakers should not have to make an effort to understand accented English.

AFFIRMATIVE ACTION: Policy that strives for increased minority enrollment, activity, or membership, often with the intention of diversifying a certain environment such as a school or workplace.

AFROCENTRISM: Intellectual position grounded in African values and ethos.

AMERICANIZATION: Effort by social workers to teach immigrants American customs, diets, and hygiene.

AMICUS BRIEF: Friend-of-the-court document usually filed by an organization with an interest in a case.

ANTI-SEMITISM: Attitude or behavior that is discriminatory toward Jewish people.

ANTISNITCHING CAMPAIGNS: Informal pressures not to cooperate with the police in investigating crimes.

APARTHEID: Official separation of the races, as formerly in South Africa.

ARYAN RACE: Term applied to white people of northern European descent; often used to imply white supremacy.

ASSIMILATION: Process of taking on social and cultural traits of the majority race in the nation in which one resides.

AVERSIVE RACISM: Attempts to avoid people of color or to be formal, correct, and cold in dealings with them.

BARRIO: Latino neighborhood.

BICULTURAL EDUCATION: Pedagogical approach that encourages retention of a child's original or family culture.

BILINGUALISM: Policy that emphasizes preservation of native languages.

BINARY PARADIGM OF RACE: Pattern of framing race issues in terms of two categories, such as black and white.

BIOLOGICAL VIEW OF RACE: Once popular view that humanity is divided into four or five major groups, corresponding to objective and real physical differences.

BIRACIAL IDENTITY: Identity of a person whose heritage or culture encompasses more than one category.

BIRTHRIGHT CITIZENSHIP: Status of persons born in the United States who automatically become citizens irrespective of their parents' legal status.

BLACK PANTHERS: Radical Black Power organization that sprang up in the 1960s and rejected integration and nonviolent change.

BLACK RAGE: Legal defense notion, as yet unrecognized, holding that a criminal action that results from understandable racial anger or indignation should qualify for a partial excuse.

BLACK-WHITE BINARY: Binary paradigm that considers the black-white relationship central to racial analysis.

BORDERLANDS: Southwestern lands that lie close to the United States' border with Mexico and still retain much Mexican culture and influence.

BORDER PATROL: Federal agency charged with policing the border between the United States and Mexico, as well as between the United States and Canada.

BRACERO PROGRAMS: Official programs that permit entry of temporary Mexican workers, especially for agriculture.

BROKER CLASS: Minorities, often well assimilated, educated, and light skinned, who perform tasks on behalf of dominantly white corporations, managing other minorities or helping the corporations sell products to the minority community.

CAMPUS SPEECH CODES: University and college regulations that provide for discipline of speakers who insult or demean members of the campus community.

CAPITALISM: System in which market forces dictate economic decisions and most property is privately owned.

CHICANOS/CHICANAS: Self-designation adopted by many Mexican Americans living in the United States; often a term of pride.

CHINESE EXCLUSION ACTS: Federal laws that prevented Chinese laborers from entering or reentering the United States.

CIVIL RIGHTS ACTS: Federal statutes guaranteeing nondiscrimination in employment, housing, voting, education, and similar areas.

CIVIL RIGHTS MOVEMENT: Effort to advance the interests of minority communities in achieving equal citizenship.

CLASS: Group of individuals who share a similar socioeconomic status.

COALITION POLITICS: Joint approach by minority groups in pursuit of common ends.

COGNITIVE DISSONANCE: Puzzlement at perceiving something that deviates from the expected, such as a black astrophysicist who wins the Nobel Prize, or over an inconsistency between what one knows and how one has been acting.

COLD WAR: Battle of position between the United States and the former Soviet Union that began shortly after the conclusion of World War II.

COLONIALISM: European effort to maintain control of weaker nations; the United States followed similar policy in the Philippines, the Caribbean, and Latin America.

COLOR BLINDNESS: Belief that one should treat all persons equally, without regard to their race.

COLOR IMAGERY: Words, texts, and television images that associate skin color with traits such as innocence, criminality, or physical beauty.

CONSERVATIVE BACKLASH: Reaction of some persons and corporations to civil rights gains, often including campaigns against welfare, affirmative action, and immigration.

CONTRADICTION-CLOSING CASE: Judicial decision handed down to conceal a widening gap between our ideals and the actual situation in the world, often the product of injustice.

CORRIDO: Latino folk song or lament, recounting a tale of heroic resistance or bravery in the face of danger.

COUNTERMAJORITARIANISM: View that the court system is free to strike down laws enacted by the majority that are unfair to minority groups.

COUNTERSTORYTELLING: Writing that aims to cast doubt on the validity of accepted premises or myths, especially ones held by the majority.

CRITICAL LEGAL STUDIES: Legal movement that challenged liberalism from the Left, denying that law is neutral, that every case has a single correct answer, and that rights are of vital importance.

CRITICAL RACE FEMINISM: Application of critical race theory to issues of concern to women of color.

CRITICAL RACE MASCULINISM: Application of critical race theory to the construction of male norms in society.

CRITICAL RACE THEORY: Progressive legal movement that seeks to transform the relationship among race, racism, and power.

CRITIQUE OF RIGHTS: Critical legal studies position that rights are alienating, ephemeral, and much less useful than most people think.

CULTURAL DEFENSE: Criminal law strategy that shows that the accused's crime was acceptable in his or her culture.

CUMULATIVE VOTING: Reform in which voters may cast as many votes as positions up for election and may concentrate them on one individual if they choose.

DECONSTRUCTION: Intellectual approach that targets traditional interpretations of terms, concepts, and practices, showing that they contain unsuspected meanings or internal contradictions.

DEPORTATION: Process by which undocumented persons are expelled to their nation of origin.

DESEGREGATION: Policy to integrate the races in schools or housing.

DETERMINISM: View that individuals and culture are products of particular forces, such as economics, biology, or the search for high status.

DIFFERENTIAL RACIALIZATION: Process by which each racial and ethnic group comes to be viewed and treated differently by mainstream society.

DISCOURSE: Formal, extensive, oral or written treatment of a subject; the way we speak about something.

DISCRIMINATION: Practice of treating similarly situated individuals differently because of race, gender, sexual orientation, appearance, or national origin.

DISENFRANCHISEMENT: Process by which citizens are deprived of voting or other rights of citizenship, for example, as a result of a felony conviction ("felon disenfranchisement").

DIVERSITY: Policy founded on the belief that individuals of different races and ethnicities can contribute to workplaces, schools, and other settings.

DOUBLE CONSCIOUSNESS: Notion attributed to W. E. B. Du Bois that black folks are able to see racial events from two perspectives—that of the majority group and their own—at the same time.

DREAMERS: Children of undocumented parents who have spent most of their lives in the United States but are not

U.S. citizens and seek to remain here legally, for example, to enroll in college.

DRIVING WHILE BLACK: Term for police practice of singling out minority drivers for special attention, such as by pulling them over and searching for drugs or contraband. See also Profiling.

EDUCATION, CRITICAL RACE THEORY IN: Scholarly movement that applies critical race theory to issues in the field of education, including high-stakes testing, affirmative action, hierarchy in schools, tracking and school discipline, bilingual and multicultural education, and the debate over ethnic studies and the Western canon.

EMPATHIC FALLACY: Mistaken belief that sweeping social reform can be accomplished through speech and incremental victories within the system.

ENGLISH-ONLY MOVEMENT: Movement that seeks to require the use of English solely in government services, voting, schools, and other settings.

EPITHETS: Pejoratives or slurs used to demean another person or group.

EQUAL EMPLOYMENT OPPORTUNITY COMMISSION (EEOC): Federal agency charged with investigating employment discrimination.

EQUAL PROTECTION CLAUSE: Part of the Fourteenth Amendment to the U.S. Constitution that requires that states treat citizens equally.

ERASURE: Practice of collective indifference to the identity, history, stories, and culture of a group, rendering them invisible.

ESSENTIALISM: Search for the unique essence of a group.

ETHNICITY: Group characteristic often based on national origin, ancestry, language, or other cultural characteristic or pattern.

EUGENICS: Attempt to better the quality of the human race through means such as sterilization, selective breeding, or mass extermination.

EUROCENTRISM: Tendency to interpret the world in terms of European values and perspectives and the belief that they are superior.

EXCEPTIONALISM: Belief that a particular group's history justifies treating it as unique and special.

FALSE CONSCIOUSNESS: Phenomenon in which oppressed people internalize and identify with attitudes and ideology of the controlling class.

FARMWORKERS' MOVEMENT: Organization spearheaded by César Chávez in the 1960s to improve health and safety standards and employment opportunities for farmworkers, including migrants.

FIRST AMENDMENT: Amendment to the U.S. Constitution that provides for freedom of speech, religion, and assembly.

FORMAL EQUALITY: Belief that the law should only provide treatment and opportunity that are the same for all.

FOURTEENTH AMENDMENT: Amendment to the U.S. Constitution that provides for equal protection and due process.

GAY BASHING: Violence or harsh words aimed at gays and lesbians.

GAY/LESBIAN (LGBT) OR QUEER LEGAL THEORY: Theory that places sexual orientation and liberation at the center of analysis.

GREASER: Derogatory term for Mexicans or Chicanos.

GREEN CARD: Identification card proving that a non-citizen is a permanent legal resident within the United States.

HATE CRIME: A crime motivated by bias based on race, religion, color, national origin, sexual orientation, or other category designated by law.

HATE SPEECH: Racial slurs and epithets or other harsh language that has no purpose other than to demean and marginalize other people or groups.

HEGEMONY: Domination by the ruling class and unconscious acceptance of that state of affairs by the subordinate group.

HETEROSEXISM: Preference for straight relationships and view that same-sex ones are unnatural.

HIP-HOP THEORY: Approach to racial justice that borrows ideas and attitudes from popular culture, especially rap music.

HIRING QUOTAS: Policy of setting aside a specific number of slots or jobs for certain groups or people.

HISPANIC: Term for persons of Iberian or Spanish ancestry; now less commonly used than the terms "Latino" or "Chicano."

HOMOPHOBIA: Prejudice against lesbians and gays.

HYPODESCENT: "One-drop rule" that holds that anyone with any degree of discernible African ancestry is black.

IDENTITY: That by which one defines oneself, such as straight, college educated, Filipina.

IDEOLOGY: Set of strongly held beliefs or values, especially dealing with governance of society.

ILLEGAL ALIEN: Pejorative term for undocumented worker, that is, one who works in the United States without holding official papers.

IMMIGRANT ANALOGY: Belief that racialized minority groups, especially Latinos and Asians, will follow the same path of assimilation as white European ethnics.

IMMIGRATION AND NATURALIZATION SERVICE (INS): Federal agency formerly charged with enforcing immigration laws; its functions have now been taken up by the Department of Homeland Security.

IMMIGRATION REFORM: Collection of proposals to lessen undocumented entry, provide a path to citizenship, and "gain control over our borders."

IMPERIALISM: Political and economic domination of one nation or group over another.

IMPLICIT BIAS: Unconscious association of one idea with another, such as race and personal qualities, frequently evincing a negative attitude.

INDETERMINACY: Idea that legal reasoning rarely, if ever, has exactly one right answer and that politics and social pressures on judges influence outcomes.

INDIAN REMOVAL: Policy of relocating eastern Native American tribes to lands west of the Mississippi so that white settlers could take over their homelands.

INITIATIVE PROCESS: Direct democracy by which citizens

vote for laws without the intervention of their elected representatives.

INTEGRATION: Process of desegregating environments such as public schools or neighborhoods.

INTEREST CONVERGENCE: Thesis pioneered by Derrick Bell that the majority group tolerates advances for racial justice only when it suits its interest to do so.

INTERNAL COLONIALISM: View that some domestic minority groups, particularly Mexicans and Puerto Ricans, are for all intents and purposes internal colonies of the United States.

INTERNMENT: Forced confinement of West Coast Japanese Americans in relocation camps during World War II.

INTERSECTIONALITY: Belief that individuals and classes often have shared or overlapping interests or traits.

JIM CROW LAWS: Antiloitering laws, poll taxes, sundown provisions, and other measures enacted, usually in the South, in order to maintain white superiority even after slavery came to an end.

JUDICIAL REVIEW: Policy under which courts determine whether laws are constitutional.

JURY NULLIFICATION: Process by which a jury acquits a defendant even though the law would technically require conviction.

KU KLUX KLAN: White-supremacist organization originating in the nineteenth-century South that has employed lynching, cross burnings, parades, and terrorism to intimidate African Americans, Mexicans, Catholics, and Jews.

LATCRIT (LATINO-CRITICAL) THEORY: Branch of critical race theory that considers issues of concern to Latinos, such as immigration, language rights, and multi-identity.

LATINOS/LATINAS: Persons of Latin American ancestry residing in the United States; sometimes called "Hispanic."

LEGAL DOCTRINE: Rule of law derived from a legislative enactment or judicial opinion.

LEGAL REALISM: Early-twentieth-century forerunner of critical legal studies that disavowed mechanical jurisprudence in favor of social science, politics, and policy judgment.

LEGAL STORYTELLING AND NARRATIVE: Using stories, parables, and first-person accounts to understand and analyze racial issues.

LEGITIMACY: Quality of an institution, such as the law, that is viewed as justified and worthy of respect.

LIBERALISM: Political philosophy that holds that the purpose of government is to maximize liberty; in civil rights, the view that law should enforce formal equality in treatment of all citizens.

MAJORITARIANISM: View that majority culture and attitudes should hold sway.

MANIFEST DESTINY: Mid-nineteenth-century ideology holding that U.S. territorial expansion was inevitable and just.

MAQUILADORAS: Assembly plants set up by U.S. corporations just inside the Mexican border to take advantage of cheap labor and lax workplace and environmental regulations.

MARKETPLACE OF IDEAS: Notion that free exchange of ideas best promotes truth and good government.

MARXISM: Political, social, and economic doctrine of Karl Marx, in particular the view that capitalism exploits workers and promotes inequality.

MELTING POT: Assimilation metaphor holding that individuals and groups blend together to create a new society.

MERIT: Conventional worthiness—concept that critical race scholars call into question because they hold that it is unfair to rank people according to mechanical scales and distribute valuable social benefits on that basis.

MESTIZOS/MESTIZAS: Person of mixed European and Indian ancestry, especially in countries that were once colonized by Spain.

MICROAGGRESSION: Stunning small encounter with racism, usually unnoticed by members of the majority race.

MIGRANT WORKER: Individual who moves from region to region to find work, especially in harvesting crops.

MINDSET: State of mind or attitude, often unconscious.

MISCEGENATION: Marriage or cohabitation between individuals of different races; formerly prohibited by law when one of the parties was white.

MODEL MINORITY MYTH: Idea that Asian Americans are hardworking, intelligent, and successful and that other groups should emulate them.

MULTICULTURALISM: View that social institutions should reflect many cultures.

MULTIPLE CONSCIOUSNESS: Ability of people of color to perceive something in two or more ways, for example, as a member of his or her group would see it and as a white would. See also Double consciousness.

MULTIRACIAL CATEGORY: A category for people with mixed racial background that many people think the U.S. Census should provide.

MULTIRACIAL PERSON: Individual whose ancestry includes persons of different races.

NAFTA: North American Free Trade Agreement that allows American corporations access to Mexican and Canadian markets.

NATIONALISM: View that a minority group should focus on its own affairs and interests first.

NATIVISM: View that the United States should give priority to its current citizenry and limit immigration.

NATURALIZATION: Process of becoming a U.S. citizen.

NEGROPHOBE: One who irrationally fears or dislikes African Americans.

NEOCOLONIALISM: View that society is taking on the structure of a colonial society, with an occupying group maintaining control over a large but diffuse group, usually of color.

NORMATIVE: Of, pertaining to, or based on a norm, especially one regarded as broad or universal.

ONE-DROP RULE: Rule of hypodescent, that any person with discernible black ancestry is black and can never be white.

OPERATION WETBACK: Government policy instituted in 1954–1959 under which as many as 3.7 million Mexicans and Mexican Americans were deported, in violation of their civil liberties.

PARADIGM: Reigning system of belief that controls what is seen as possible, relevant, and valid.

PASSING: Crossing the color line and gaining acceptance into a race other than one's original one.

PATRIARCHY: System of beliefs and practices in which men dominate and control women.

PERSPECTIVALISM: Belief that a person's or group's position or standpoint greatly influences how they see truth and reality.

PLENARY POWER DOCTRINE: Judicial view that congressional enactments concerning immigration are unreviewable by courts because Congress's power in this area is unlimited.

POPULIST MOVEMENT: Movement that focuses on the common people or workers.

POSTMODERNISM: Critique of modernism, a previous system founded on Enlightenment thinking and philosophy, and capitalism.

POSTRACIAL: The condition of being beyond race; an era when race no longer matters.

POSTSTRUCTURALISM: Critique of structuralism, an earlier movement that aimed to determine basic structural elements of social systems, especially in the social and behavioral sciences.

PREJUDICE: Belief or attitude, usually unfavorable, about a person or group before the facts are known; a prejudgment.

PRINCIPLE OF INVOLUNTARY SACRIFICE: Notion, attributed to Derrick Bell, that the costs of civil rights advances are always placed on blacks or low-income whites.

PRIVILEGE: Right or advantage, often unwritten, conferred on some people but not others, usually without examination or good reason.

PROFILING: Practice in which the authorities single out ethnic or racial minority persons for heightened suspicion or detention. See also Driving while black.

PROPERTY INTEREST IN WHITENESS: Idea that white skin and identity are economically valuable. See also Whiteness as property.

PUBLIC-PRIVATE DISTINCTION: Notion that many types of law operate only in the public sector, for example, that one is free to rent a room in one's personal home to anyone one wants.

PUSH-PULL THEORY OF MIGRATION: Idea that Mexicans come to the United States in accordance with the demand of the U.S. labor market or in response to adverse conditions in Mexico.

RACE: Notion of a distinct biological type of human being, usually based on skin color or other physical characteristics.

RACE TRAITOR: A white person who identifies as black in an effort to subvert white privilege and tacit assumptions that underlie racism.

RACIAL FRAUD AND BOX CHECKING: Action on the part of a nonminority person, or one with a very slight connection with a minority group, to gain the benefit of minority status, as with affirmative action.

RACIALIZATION: Process of creating a race, such as Latinos; also injecting a racial element into a situation. See also Differential racialization.

RACIAL REALISM: View that racial progress is sporadic and that people of color are doomed to experience only infrequent peaks followed by regressions.

RACISM: Any program or practice of discrimination, segregation, persecution, or mistreatment based on membership in a race or ethnic group.

REASONABLE RACIST: One who treats members of another group in racist fashion because he or she believes that, statistically, the other group is prone to crime or similar behavior.

RECONSTRUCTION: Period when society is attempting to redress racial wrongs consistently and in thoroughgoing fashion.

REDISTRICTING: Process of redrawing geographical lines of political districts to achieve fairness in voting.

REDLINING: Policy by insurance companies, banks, and mortgage lenders not to do business with home buyers or owners in certain areas with heavy minority population.

REPARATIONS: Forms of compensation, such as money, given to a group or class of individuals who have been wronged.

RESTRICTIVE COVENANTS: Legally enforceable limitation on land use or occupancy, often created by the original home owner or developer of neighborhoods.

REVERSE DISCRIMINATION: Discrimination aimed at the majority group.

REVISIONIST INTERPRETATION: View of history or an event that challenges the accepted one.

RULE OF LAW: Legal formalism, which some theorists

believe is necessary for order, stability, and cohesiveness in a society.

SEGREGATION: Separation of individuals or groups by race.

SEPARATE-BUT-EQUAL DOCTRINE: Rule of law holding that separate but equal facilities for different races are constitutional under the Equal Protection Clause.

SEPARATISM: View that a racial minority group should separate itself from mainstream society and pursue its own interests primarily. See also Nationalism.

SILENCING: Practice or speech that interferes with the ability of others to communicate.

SOCIAL CONSTRUCTION: Process of endowing a group or concept with a delineation, name, or reality.

STANDING: Rule that limits the person who may bring a lawsuit to the one who suffered the "injury in fact."

STATUS QUO: Current state, the way things are—usually said to require a good reason before it is changed.

STEREOTYPE: Fixed, usually negative, image of members of a group.

STEREOTYPE THREAT: Tendency of test-takers to perform poorly if they are conscious that an examination may confirm a widespread social image of them as intellectually inferior.

STIGMATIZATION: Process of marking a person, thing, or group as an object of shame or disgrace.

STOCK STORIES: Tales that a people commonly subscribe to and use to explain their social reality, for example, that African Americans who try hard will be accepted and succeed, or that Mexican immigrants will take black jobs.

STRUCTURAL DETERMINISM: Concept that a mode of

thought or a widely shared practice determines significant social outcomes, usually without our conscious knowledge.

SUBORDINATION: Process of rendering a particular group of lesser importance, as through racial discrimination, patriarchy, or classism.

SWEATSHOP: Factory where workers, such as recent immigrants or Third World women, work under unsafe conditions, often for low pay.

TERRA NULLIUS: British doctrine according to which colonial land belonged to the settling nation. See also Manifest Destiny.

TITLE VII: Federal law that governs employment discrimination.

TRAIL OF TEARS: Route used for forced removal of certain Native American nations from the southeastern United States to lands west of the Mississippi River. See also Indian removal.

TRANSPARENCY: Tendency of whiteness to disguise itself and become invisible.

TRIBAL SOVEREIGNTY: View that American Indian nations and tribes are separate political entities (nations) and entitled to treatment as such.

UNCONSCIOUS RACISM: Racism that operates at an unconscious or subtle level.

UNDOCUMENTED WORKER: U.S. immigrant who has not obtained legal status.

VIGILANTE: An individual who sets out to enforce the law on his or her own and without official authorization, for example, a border vigilante.

VOICE: Ability of a group, such as African Americans or women, to articulate experience in ways unique to it.

WASP: Term for persons of white, Anglo-Saxon, Protestant descent.

WHITENESS: Quality pertaining to Euro-American or Caucasian people or traditions.

WHITENESS AS PROPERTY: Notion that whiteness itself has value for its possessor and conveys a host of privileges and benefits. See also Property interest in whiteness.

Index

accent discrimination, 78, 84, 94, 128; definition of, 167

Acuña, Rodolfo, and nationalism, 69

affirmative action, 130–135; and class, 119; critique of, 131–132; defense of, 132; definition of, 167; and white privilege, 91

African Americans: and environmental justice, 116–118; and home ownership, 116, 117, 119

Afrocentrism, definition of, 167

Aguilar v. Avis Rent a Car System, Inc., 106

Alfieri, Anthony, and stories in clinical lawyering, 53

Americanization, definition of, 167

amicus brief, definition of, 167

antiessentialism, 10–11; and Latinos, 93. *See also* essentialism/antiessentialism debate

anti-Semitism, definition of, 167

antisnitching campaigns, 62; definition of, 167

apartheid, definition of, 167

Arizona: and English only laws, 128–129; and high school ethnic studies programs, 68–69, 129; and laws against undocumented people, 129

Aryan race, definition of, 168

Asians: and critical legal theory, 3, 94–96; model minority stereotype, 94; and whiteness, 82

assimilation, 66–70; definition of, 168

aversive racism, definition of, 168

Avis. See *Aguilar v. Avis Rent a Car System, Inc.*

Aztlan, 69

Bakke, Alan, and affirmative action, 38, 131

barrio, definition of, 168

beauty, standards of, 83, 142

Bell, Derrick, xv, 4, 6, 9, 22–24, 35, 38, 45, 48, 68, 104, 108, 140

Bell Curve, The, and affirmative action, 131–132

bicultural education, definition of, 168

bilingualism, definition of, 168

binary paradigm of race: definition of, 168; historical harms of, 80–82. *See also* black-white binary

biological view of race, definition of, 168. *See also* race

biracial identity: definition of, 168. *See also* multiracial

birthright citizenship, definition of, 168

black exceptionalism. *See* exceptionalism

black judges, and racial injustice, 12, 46

Black Lives Matter, 124

Black Panthers, definition of, 168

black rage, definition of, 168

black-white binary, 77–84, 93; consequences of, 80–83; definition of, 169.

black women, and dilemma of intersectionality, 59–61

book banning, in Tucson school district, 68–69

Border Patrol, definition of, 169

borderlands, definition of, 169

box checking, 83. *See also* racial fraud

bracero programs, definition of, 169

broker class, definition of, 169. *See also* minority middle managers

Brown v. Board of Education, 9, 22–24, 29, 130

Buffalo Soldiers, 82

Butler, Paul, 6, 124

buying a car, 2

California, and Proposition 187, 82

campus speech codes, definition of, 169. *See also* hate speech

capitalism, 135–136; definition of, 169. *See also* class; economic democracy; hypercapitalism

Carbado, Devon, 6, 74, 106, 154

Carino v. University of Oklahoma, 84

categorical thinking: and identity, 140; and intersectionality, 58–64; and race, 21, 32–33, 79, 140–141; and whiteness, 85. *See also* black-white binary

Chicanos/Chicanas, definition of, 169

Chin, Vincent, 94

Chinese Exclusion Acts, 81; definition of, 169

citizenship, racial qualification for, 86–88

Civil Rights Acts, definition of, 169

civil rights discourse, and critical race theory, 3, 5–6. *See also* liberalism; rights

civil rights movement, definition of, 170

class, 106–107; and affirmative action, 133–135; definition of, 170; intersection of race and, 115–120; theory of, 115–116

classism, and beggar story, 19–20

classroom exercises, 35, 37, 70, 92, 109, 142, 160

coalition politics, 83–84; definition of, 170; and globalization, 117, 136–137

Cochran, Johnny, 53
cognitive dissonance, definition of, 170
Cold War, 23; definition of, 170
colonialism: definition of, 170; effect on globalization, 136; legacy of, 136–137
color blindness, 8–9; and affirmative action, 130–135; and the Constitution, 26; definition of, 170; and judging, 12, 26–28; and racial remedies, 26–28
color consciousness in judicial decisions, 26–28
color imagery, 85–86; definition of, 170
Commonwealth v. Local Union 542, International Union of Operating Engineers, 12, 46
conservative(s): and affirmative action, 131–132; agenda, 30; campaigns, 104, 114; definition of, backlash, 170
contradiction-closing cases, 38; definition of, 170
corrido, definition of, 171
countermajoritarianism, definition of, 171
counterstorytelling, 49–50; definition of, 171; power of, 50–53; about racial subordination, 48–49. *See also* legal storytelling and narrative
covering, 74
Crenshaw, Kimberlé, xv, 6
crime: defining, 120–121; white collar, 50, 121
criminal justice system, and minorities, 120–124

critical legal studies: and critical race theory, 5, 158; definition of, 171
critical race feminism, 96; definition of, 171
critical race masculinism, definition of, 171
critical race theory: and activism, 8, 105–106; and affirmative action, 119–120; and charge of anti-Semitism, 103; and class, 115–120; and color blindness, 27–28; and conservative campaigns, 104, 114; and context, 65; and critical legal studies, 5; criticism of, 102–109; and critique of merit, 103–104, 132–135; definition of, 3, 171; and economic democracy, 108; in education, 7, 173; and empirical analysis, 142–144; and ethnic studies, 6; and feminism, 5; front-burner issues of, 114–140; future of, 152–161; and identity, 106–108, 140–142; and interest convergence, 20–24; internal critique of, 104–108; and legal indeterminacy, 5; and legal storytelling, 44–54; and liberalism, 5, 6, 22, 26–31, 64–65; and material determinism, 20–24, 81–82; and nationalism, 67–69; origins of, xv–xvii, 3–4; and philosophy, 8; principal figures in, 6–7; and racial realism, 20–24; relations within, 106–108, 140–142; and relationship to previous movements, 5–6;

critical race theory (*continued*)
   and relevance outside U.S.,
   108–109; and revisionist
   history, 25–26; and social construction of race, 9, 21; spin-
   off movements of, 3–4, 7–8;
   and spread to other countries,
   8, 108–109; and structural
   determinism, 31–39; tenets of,
   8–11; themes of, 19–39; and
   theory, 105–106
critical white studies, 85–92
critique of liberalism. *See* liberalism, critique of
critique of merit. *See* merit,
   critique of
critique of rights. *See* rights,
   critique of
cultural defense, definition of,
   171
culture of poverty. *See* poverty
cummings, andré, 7
cumulative voting, 139; definition of, 171. *See also* voting

darkness, associated with evil, 86
Dawes Act, 81
deconstruction, definition of, 171
Delgado, Richard, xv, 4, 26, 50,
   102, 157
deportation, definition of, 172
desegregation, definition of, 172
determinism, definition of, 172.
   See also material determinism;
   structural determinism
differend, 51–52
differential racialization, 9–10,
   74–80; definition of, 172.
   See also racialization
discourse, definition of, 172

discrimination: accent, 78, 84,
   94, 128, 167; definition of,
   172; difficulty of intersectional claim of, 59–63; failure
   of colorblind programs to
   redress, 65, 119–122; housing, 115–116, 117; and legal
   storytelling, 50–51; proxy,
   93; reverse, 91, 183; statistical, 121; workplace, 59–62,
   106, 144, 185. *See also*
   oppression
disenfranchisement, definition
   of, 172; felon, 124, 139, 155.
   See also voting
diversity, definition of, 172
double consciousness, 46, definition of, 172
double minorities, 65
dreamers, 93; definition of, 172
Driver, Justin, 108
driving while black, definition of,
   173. *See also* racial profiling
Du Bois, W. E. B., and double
   consciousness, 46
Dudziak, Mary, 23–24

economic democracy, 108, 156.
   See also class
economic determinism. *See* material determinism
education, critical race theory
   in: definition of, 173; development of, 7
empathic fallacy, 33–35; definition of, 173
empathy, 33–35, 48; and sentencing, 35
empirical analysis, and racial
   oppression, 142–144

employment discrimination. *See* discrimination: workplace; Title VII

English-only movement: definition of, 173; statutes, 128–129

environmental justice movement, 116–118

epithets, definition of, 173. *See also* hate speech; racial insults

Equal Employment Opportunity Commission (EEOC), definition of, 173

Equal Protection Clause, 130; definition of, 173

equality, colorblind, 8

erasure, definition of, 173

essentialism, 63–64; definition of, 173

essentialism/antiessentialism debate, 63–66. *See also* antiessentialism

ethnicity, definition of, 174

eugenics, definition of, 174

Eurocentrism, definition of, 174

European Americans, and whiteness, 88–89

"everything must change at once," 91

exceptionalism: black, 79; and coalitions, 83; definition of, 174

exclusion of minority scholarship, 102–103

false consciousness, definition of, 174

Farber, Daniel, and critique of critical race theory, 54, 102–104

farmworkers' movement, definition of, 174

feminism, and critical race theory, 5. *See also* critical race feminism

First Amendment: definition of, 174; and speech rights, 29, 106, 125–126, 128–129

formal equality, definition of, 174

Fourteenth Amendment, definition of, 174

Freeman, Alan, 4, 6, 38

Gallo. See People ex rel. Joan Gallo v. Acuna

gangs, 121–122

gay bashing, definition of, 174

gay/lesbian (LGBT) or queer legal theory, 96–97, definition of, 175

Gertner, Judge Nancy, 123

globalization, 135–137; and possibility of worldwide worker coalitions, 136–137

Gómez, Laura, 6

Gotanda, Neil, 6

greaser, definition of, 175. *See also* hate speech

green card, definition of, 175

Greene County boot camp, 28

Grutter v. Bollinger, 131, 135, 143

Guinier, Lani, 6, 106, 157

Gulati, Mitu, 6, 74, 106, 154

Haney López, Ian, 6, 49, 85

Harlan, Justice John: and the Chinese, 82; and dissent in *Plessy v. Ferguson*, 26–27, 130

Harris, Angela, xiii–xvii, 6
Harris, Cheryl, 6, 85
Harvard Law School, xv
hate crime, definition of, 175
hate speech, 33–34, 125–128;
    and *Aguilar v. Avis Rent a Car
    System, Inc.*, 106; and campus
    climate, 127; definition of,
    175; on the Internet, 127–128;
    jurisprudence in Canada, 125–
    126; and *Monteiro v. Tempe
    Union High School District*,
    38–39; remedies for, 125–126;
    and *Taylor v. Metzger*, 26, 80,
    126–127; and *Words That
    Wound*, 26
hegemony, 46–47; definition of,
    175
heterosexism, definition of, 175
Higginbotham, Judge Leon, 12,
    46
hip-hop theory: and criminal law,
    124; definition of, 175
Hirabayashi v. United States,
    93–94
hiring quotas, definition of, 175
Hispanic, definition of, 175
homeostasis, and law reform, 38
homophobia, definition of, 175
hydra, two-headed, of race, 90
hypercapitalism, 108, 136. *See
    also* capitalism
hypodescent, definition of, 175

idealists: and identity, 140–142;
    and social construction of
    race, 9, 21; and strategies for
    law reform, 25–26
identity, 10–11, 107–108, 140–
    142; definition of, 176

ideology, definition of, 176
illegal alien, definition of, 176
immigrant analogy, definition
    of, 176
Immigration and Naturalization
    Service (INS), definition of,
    176
immigration: activism, 93;
    enforcement, 129; law and
    policy, 86–88, 137–138; and
    probable cause laws, 93;
    reform, definition of, 176; and
    whiteness, 86–89
imperialism, definition of, 176
Implicit Association Test (IAT),
    13; use of, 143
implicit bias, 13, 143–144; defi-
    nition of, 176
indeterminacy, legal, 5; definition
    of, 176
Indian Appropriation Act, 81
Indian removal, definition of,
    176
indigenous movements: and peo-
    ple's rights, 3; and resistance
    to hypercapitalism, 136–137
initiative process, definition of,
    176
integration, definition of, 177
interest convergence, 9, 20–24,
    48; critique of, 108; defini-
    tion of, 177; and demographic
    shift, 154; and Derrick Bell,
    22–24, 108
internal colonialism, 69; defini-
    tion of, 177; and location of
    biohazards, 116
internment, definition of, 177.
    See also Japanese Americans
interracial. *See* multiracial

intersectionality, 10–11, 58–63, 96; and claims for discrimination, 59–61; definition of, 177; of race and poverty, 119; and women's studies, 159

Japanese Americans: internment of, 83, 94–95; and reparations, 95; and whiteness requirement for citizenship, 86–88
Jersey Heights Neighborhood Ass'n v. Glendening, 117–118
Jim Crow laws, definition of, 177
Johnson, Kevin, 6
Johnson, Lyndon (Pres.), 131
judicial review, definition of, 177
jury nullification, 122; definition of, 177

Kang, Jerry, 6
Kennedy, Randall, and critique of critical race theory, 102–103; response to, by critical race scholars, 103
King, Martin Luther, Jr., 130
Korematsu v. United States, and NAACP, 83
Ku Klux Klan, definition of, 177
Kuhn, Thomas, 51

language rights, 125–129
LatCrit theory, 3, 93; definition of, 178
Latino/a critical legal theory. *See* LatCrit theory
Latinos/Latinas: and black-white binary, 78, 82, 93; definition of, 178; and identity, 141; issues, 92–93; and nationalism, 68–69; and nativism, 93

law reform: and counterstorying, 48; and homeostasis, 38; idealist strategies for, 25–26, 140–141; and legal research tools, 32–33; materialist strategies for, 25, 140, 141
Lawrence, Charles, 6, 106, 157
lawyering for social change, 36–37
legal concepts and categories, 32–33
legal doctrine, definition of, 178
legal realism, 126; definition of, 178
legal research tools, as hindrances to law reform, 32–33
legal storytelling and narrative, 11, 44–54; in court, 52–53; critique of, 53–54; definition of, 178; interpretations of, 44–45; power of, 50–53; use of, 45–46, 50–51. *See also* counterstorytelling; narratives and narrative theory
legitimacy, definition of, 178
lesbian legal theory. *See* gay/lesbian (LGBT) or queer legal theory
Levit, Nancy, 7
LGBT legal theory. *See* gay/lesbian (LGBT) or queer legal theory
liberalism: critique of, 22, 26–31, 64–65; definition of, 178
look-to-the-bottom strategy, 27
López, Gerald, 7
López, Ian Haney. *See* Haney López, Ian
Lowell High School (San Francisco, Calif.), and admissions, 83

LSAT (Law School Admissions
    Test), 132, 135, 143; and
    stereotype threat, 142–143
Lyotard, Jean-François, 51–52

majoritarianism, definition of,
    178
Manifest Destiny, definition of,
    178
maquiladoras, 136; definition
    of, 178
marketplace of ideas, definition
    of, 179
Martinez, George, 51
Marxism, definition of, 179
material determinism, 9,
    20–24, 81. *See also* interest
    convergence
materialists: and nationalism,
    67–68; and revisionist history,
    25; and strategies for law
    reform, 25, 140, 141; and
    white self-interest, 21–22
Matsuda, Mari, xv, 6, 106, 127,
    157
McIntosh, Peggy, and white
    privilege, 90
melting pot, definition of, 179
merit: critique of, 103–104, 132–
    135; definition of, 179
mestizos/mestizas, definition of,
    179
Mexican Americans: effect of
    U.S. war with Mexico on,
    81; and other white policy,
    82, 83
microaggressions, 1–3, 144;
    definition of, 179
Middle Easterners, 4, 115;
    stereotypes of, 10, 52

migrant worker, definition of,
    179
mindset, 50, 77; definition of,
    179
minority middle managers, 83,
    154–155. *See also* broker class
miscegenation, definition of, 179
mixed race. *See* multiracial
model minority myth, 94; defini-
    tion of, 179
*Monteiro v. Tempe Union High
    School District*, 38–39
Montoya, Margaret, 6
multiculturalism, definition of,
    179
multiple consciousness, 63; defi-
    nition of, 179
multiracial: and the Census,
    71–72, 93, 141; definition of,
    category, 180; definition of,
    person, 180; identity, 71–72,
    141, 152–153
Muslims, animus against, 4, 24,
    82, 115

NAACP: and *Korematsu v.
    United States*, 83; Legal
    Defense Fund and *Brown*, 22
NAFTA, 136; definition of, 180
narratives and narrative theory,
    34–35, 44–54; in court, 52–
    53; and the *differend*, 51–52;
    and mindset, 50. *See also* legal
    storytelling and narrative
nationalism, 66–70; black, 66–
    68; definition of, 180; Latino,
    68–69
nativism, 93; definition of, 180
naturalization: definition of, 180;
    and race cases, 86–89

negrophobe, definition of, 180
neocolonialism, definition of, 180
nomos, and narrative theory, 49
normative, definition of, 180

Obama, Barack (Pres.), xix, 24,
    26, 30, 51, 89, 104
one-drop rule, definition of, 180
Onwuachi-Willig, Angela, 6
Operation Wetback, definition
    of, 180
oppression: economic, 13, 107–
    108, 136; hydra of, 90; and
    implicit bias, 144; and inter-
    sectionality, 58–59; and social
    change, 63–64; and social
    dominance theory, 144; and
    stereotype threat, 142–143;
    and voice of color, 11. See also
    discrimination
Ozawa. See Takao Ozawa v.
    United States

paradigm, 51; black-white, 77–
    84; definition of, 181
passing, 69; definition of, 181
patriarchy, definition of, 181
People ex rel. Joan Gallo v.
    Acuna, 121–122
Perea, Juan, 6, 106
performative identity, 74,
    162–163
perspectivalism: definition of,
    181; and intersectionality, 62;
    and white transparency, 91
plenary power doctrine, and
    immigration, 137; definition
    of, 181
Plessy v. Ferguson, 26–27, 82,
    130

police and policing, 120–121,
    129; and community relations,
    124; and probable cause laws,
    93; racial profiling, 121–122
politics of identification, 62
politics of respectability, 62
populist movement, definition
    of, 181
Posner, Judge Richard: and cri-
    tique of legal storytelling, 54;
    and paradigm shifts, 51; and
    racial preferences, 28
postcolonial studies, and global-
    ization, 137
postmodernism, definition of, 181
postracial, 26, 30, 104, 115;
    definition of, 181
poststructuralism, definition of,
    181
poverty, 115–120; intersection of
    race and, 119
power: and demographic shift,
    152–161; between lawyer and
    client, 52–53; and shape of
    knowledge, 77–97
prejudice, definition of, 181
principle of involuntary sacrifice,
    definition of, 181
prisons and prison building,
    123–124
privilege, definition of, 182
profiling, definition of, 182.
    See also driving while black;
    racial profiling
property interest in whiteness,
    86; definition of, 182
public-private distinction, defini-
    tion of, 182
push-pull theory of migration,
    definition of, 182

queer-crit. *See* gay/lesbian (LGBT) or queer legal theory

race, 49; biological view of, 168; and black-white binary, 77–84; and body image, 142; and class, 115–120; definition of, 182; intersection of, and poverty, 119; social construction of, 9, 21, 184; traitor, definition of, 182
racial depiction. *See* stereotype(s)
racial epithets. *See* hate speech
racial fraud and box checking, definition of, 182. *See also* box checking
racial insults, 26, 80; and emotional distress, 80, 126–127. *See also* hate speech
racial profiling, 121, 122–123
racial progress and retrenchment, 81–84
racial realism, 20–24; definition of, 183. *See also* interest convergence
racial reform: and conservatives, 30–31; strategies for, 25–26, 64–66
racialization, definition of, 182. *See also* differential racialization
racism: and beggar story, 19–20; color-blind remedies for, 8–9, 26–28; definition of, 183; and innocence, 91–92; kinds of, 31–32; and microaggressions, 1–3, 144; ordinariness of, 8; quantity of, 11–13
realists. *See* materialists; racial realism

reasonable racist, definition of, 183
Reconstruction, definition of, 183
redistricting, definition of, 183
redlining, definition of, 183
Regents of University of California v. Bakke. *See* Bakke, Alan
reparations, 52; definition of, 183
restrictive covenants, definition of, 183
reverse discrimination, 91; definition of, 183. *See also* affirmative action
revisionist history, 25–26; definition of, 183
rights: critique of, 28–30, definition of, 171
Rosen, Jeffrey, and critique of critical race theory, 53
Ross, Tom, 7
Ruiz v. Hall, 128–129
rule of law, definition of, 183

Samaha v. Wash. St. Dept. of Tran., 144
Sander, Richard, and critique of affirmative action, 133
SAT (Scholastic Aptitude Test), 116, 132
segregation, definition of, 184
sentencing guidelines, 123–124
separate but equal, 130; definition of, 184
separatism, definition of, 184. *See also* nationalism
serving two masters, 36–37
Shelby County v. Holder, 139–140

Sherry, Suzanna, and critique of critical race theory, 55, 102–104
Sidanius, Jim, and social dominance theory, 144
silencing: cure for, 50–52, 66; definition of, 184
Simpson, O. J., verdict, 53
social construction of race. *See* race: social construction of
social dominance theory, 144
social justice. *See* racial reform
social well-being of minority groups, 12–13
standardized testing: and class, 116; critique of, 116, 132–133
standing, definition of, 184
State v. Buggs, 49
status quo, definition of, 184
Steele, Claude, and stereotype threat, 142–143
Stefancic, Jean, xvi, 7
stereotype(s): definition of, 184; of racial groups, 10, 34, 52
stereotype threat, 142–143; definition of, 184
stigmatization, definition of, 184
stock stories: about African Americans, 47; definition of, 184. *See also* legal storytelling and narrative
stories and storytelling. *See* legal storytelling and narrative
structural determinism, 31–39; definition of, 184
subordination, definition of, 185
sweatshop, 136; definition of, 185

Takao Ozawa v. United States, 87–88

Taylor v. Metzger, 26, 80, 126–127
Tea Party movement, 89
terra nullius, definition of, 185
three-strikes-and-you're-out case, 122–123
Title VII, definition of, 185
Trail of Tears, definition of, 185
transparency: definition of, 185; of whiteness, 91–92
Treaty of Guadalupe Hidalgo, 93
triangulation, politics of, 115
tribal sovereignty, definition of, 185
triumphalism, critique of, 5
Tucson, Arizona: Latino studies program banned, 68–69
Tushnet, Mark, and critique of legal storytelling, 54
unconscious racism, definition of, 185
undocumented worker, definition of, 185

United Nations, and index of social wellbeing, 13
United States: demographics of, xix, 152–153; effect of economic downturn on minorities in, 114–115; immigration policy of, 137–138; and war with Mexico, 80
United States of America v. Leviner, 123
University of California at Berkeley, and admissions, 84
University of California at Davis Medical School, and affirmative action, 131
University of Chicago, xiii–xv

U.S. Department of Justice, and school desegregation, 23–24
U.S. Department of State, and race relations, 23

Valdes, Francisco, 6
vigilante, definition of, 185
Virginia v. Black, 160
voice: of color, 11, 102; definition of, 186
voting, 139–140; cumulative, 139; and felon disenfranchisement, 124, 139, 155; and stringent requirements, 140

WASP, definition of, 186
wealth gap, 13, 118–119
Weinstein, Judge Jack B., and empathy, 35
welfare, 118
White, Lucy, and stories in clinical lawyering, 53

white collar crime, 50, 121
white privilege, 89–91; and standardized testing, 134–135
white studies. *See* critical white studies
white(s): identification of other groups with, 82, 83; and *Plessy v. Ferguson*, 26–27; supremacy groups, 89
whiteness: definition of, 186; and immigrant groups, 86–89; and innocence, 85–86, 91–92; legal definition of, 87–88; normativity of, 86, 91; as a property interest, 86, 186
Wildman, Stephanie, 7
Williams, Patricia, xv, 6, 45
Williams, Robert, 6, 158
Wittmer v. Peters, 27

Yamamoto, Eric, 6
Yoshino, Kenji, 74

About the Authors

Richard Delgado is John J. Sparkman Chair of Law at the University of Alabama and one of the founders of critical race theory. His books include *The Latino/a Condition: A Critical Reader* (coedited with Jean Stefancic; NYU Press) and *The Rodrigo Chronicles* (NYU Press).

Jean Stefancic is Professor and Clement Research Affiliate at the University of Alabama School of Law. Her books include *No Mercy: How Conservative Think Tanks and Foundations Changed America's Social Agenda*. She and Delgado edited *Critical Race Theory: The Cutting Edge*.

Made in the USA
Monee, IL
01 July 2021